CW00971340

NORTHERN ENGLAND
IN WORDS AND PICTURES

poetry *pt* today

NORTHERN ENGLAND IN WORDS AND PICTURES

Edited by Suzy Walton

First published in Great Britain in 2001 by Poetry
Today, an imprint of
Penhaligon Page Ltd, Remus House, Coltsfoot Drive,
Woodston, Peterborough. PE2 9JX

A Catalogue record for this book is available from the
British Library

ISBN 1 86226 632 8

Typesetting and layout, Penhaligon Page Ltd, England.
Printed and bound by Forward Press Ltd, England

Foreword

This book brings out the lesser known, as well as the more popular aspects of Northern England.

Poems, factual accounts, anecdotes, myths, legends and photographs all produce a fascinating picture of Northern England as it is in 2001.

Whether you already live here, or are thinking of visiting *Northern England In Words And Pictures* takes you on a delightful tour of these parts of our country.

Contents

South Yorkshire

WEST YORKSHIRE

The Hand-Loom Weaver

The last free man; beside his loom he sits and works all day
    While down below the womenfolk spin yarn and chat away.
He never fears a mill-owner; no foreman ever tells
    The hand-loom weaver how much time to make the cloth he sells.
And every week he will descend from his castle in the hills
    To Huddersfield or Halifax to settle out his bills.
A roll of cloth upon his back, and a stick to help his stride,
    Down from his cottage comes a man who plies his trade with
                                       pride.

The only worship he will give is to Him Who turns the sun
    That lightens up the weaving-loft till working-day is done;
The One Who weaves the stars in space, to Him he'll raise a hymn
    With others in the chapel there; all millstone grit and grim.
Aloof he stands and watches as the crowd flocks to the mill,
    Self-educated, he will yet harvest more knowledge still.
And though the hills should wear away in their allotted span,
    The weaver knows no king but God; he is the last free man.

Mike Smith

Leeds Lights

A flourishing business my town on the rise
not the same place that I knew as a child
Gone are the mills and going the scrublands
each giving way to new money attractions
    Where cell phones connect
    and computers collate
    in architectural perfection
    the art of the state.
Here we can dream we are free cosmopolitan
although minutes away in any direction
    is a uniform decay
    of a losing nation
    bitter, forgotten
    amid sprawling desolation.
With rat ridden squalor despair all around
unwanted bi-products of the city's rich bounds
    loosely dishevelled, brazen,
    fraud down 'n' outs
    collecting for kicks
    on streets paved with nowt.
Countless blank faces from far distant lands
call me the stranger in my home town
    a notion unknown
    to ones new and ones gone
    just a bleak reminder
    for those who belong.

Darren Hunt

Childhood Memories

I hope that some of my memories given below will be of use to you. I was born in Leeds in 1918 so remember most of what life was like in the 1920s and 30s.

I was fortunate to live in what was called a 'through house'. It had a front and back door with a yard at the back, steps down to a cellar kitchen and a lavatory of its own, built under the back doorstep and just outside the cellar door. All the houses around were 'back to backs' and shared lavatories in a yard at the end of each block. There are still many of these houses but bathrooms have been installed either in a small bedroom or the attic. The people were mostly very clean and proud of the outside of their homes, always using plenty of scouring stone on the sides of the steps.

There were regular days to do your washing as it was hung across the street but not on Sundays because these were revered as the Lord's Day. It was rubbed or scrubbed, possed, boiled, dolly blued and starched as appropriate for the materials.

In 1926 it was Tercentenary Year and to mark the occasion all Leeds school children were given a large pink bankbook with 1/- (one shilling) deposited in it. Previous to this we had little grey Yorkshire Penny Bank books in which many mothers gave their children 1d each week to take to school and save for something special.

There are several recreation areas in Leeds called 'moor', Hunslet Moor, Holbeck, Woodhouse, etc and in the summer, from the beginning of August there were fixed dates for the 'feast' held on each one, today they are called 'fun-fairs'. I lived near Hunslet Moor and ours was the first week in August. This was also August Bank Holiday and many, like my parents, struggled to save all the year round and take the family to the seaside. We usually went to Blackpool where we had a room with two double beds, one for mum and dad and the other for myself, brother and sister. Each bed cost 3/6d per night. Mum bought our own food and the landlady cooked it, except for potatoes and puddings, these were served at a small charge per portion. We were all excited on the Friday night and I remember having difficulty in going to sleep as the lights from the feast shone on our bedroom wall, flickering as the roundabouts turned.

During the 5 weeks summer holiday it was possible for children to travel on the trams for 1d return between 9am and 4pm, so in the remaining weeks of the holidays my mother would take us out one day each week, perhaps to Guiseley and we would walk to Otley, or Yeadon Dam, Roundhay Park, Temple Newsam or some other good place for children to play. She would pack sandwiches and we would have a picnic. Always the Monday before we returned to school on the Tuesday, weather permitting, we would have our last picnic.

Another annual event was Children's Day. For weeks before there were practices for dancing, gymnastic and other massed displays, area sports where the finalist competed on this day with those from other areas, a parade of decorated floats, fancy dress competition and a Queen with her four maids of honour and pages. Each school selected a girl, she was the children's choice, who went to the area final and from them a panel of judges chose one girl (there were five areas). These five girls then went before another panel who selected one as Queen and the others were then her attendants. This event was held in Roundhay Park, a natural arena for such an event, and a great day was had by all.

This arena was used for the Northern Command Tattoos before and just after the war.

Anne Lageu

New Year Nightmare In Wortley

It was 7pm on New Year's Day in 1891 and at St John's School hall it was the second evening of a Sale of Work. The hall was crowded with between sixty and eighty people, many of them were friends and relatives waiting patiently for the young performers, 'The Snowflakes', who were due to give a stage concert.

At the far end of the school hall, in a small room cluttered with tables, sewing machines and chairs, fourteen young girls giggled and chatted excitedly as they prepared. Billed as 'The Snowflakes' they were covered from head to toe in a cotton-wool costume. To get from the room on to the stage they each had to carefully climb and balance on a chair whilst carrying a Chinese Lantern, as they had successfully done at the previous evenings performance. The Chinese Lanterns had cost a penny each and had been purchased from a local shop in Wortley.

The fourteen excited little girls crowded round their tutor, Mr Eli Auty, who carefully used a taper to light each candle in the Chinese Lanterns. Whilst lighting the thirteenth candle, one girl upset her lantern and the candle fell out setting her cotton wool costume on fire. She was immediately enveloped in flames from head to toe. Tragically, within seconds, the fire spread to the other girls' costumes. Relatives and friends were horrified to hear the screams and then see the burning figures tumble on to the stage. The outer door was locked and the only means of escape was by climbing on to the chair and then the stage.

Parents and guests rushed forward to smother the flames. Some of the burned children fled out of the school rooms, trying to get home. Many of the guests fled themselves, fearing that the building was on fire. Frantic parents tried to find their children as Eli Auty, the Cannon of St John's, Cannon Brameld and his Curate Rev E F Buckton, wrapped the children in coats and rugs.

The nearby Police Station was informed and they notified the Central Fire Station, who despatched their new Ambulance. As quickly as possible, the children were taken to the Infirmary.

There were scenes of heart-rending distress as anxious parents and friends gathered at the Infirmary waiting for news.

The resident Surgeon on duty, Mr Berkeley Moynihan ~ who was later to become Lord Moynihan ~ worked with a team of other Doctors throughout the night to relieve the suffering of the children. It was reported that at about midnight nurses heard four of the little victims, now delirious, humming snatches of the songs that they would have sung in their show. By morning all four had died. In all, nine children died within the following five days. Two more were later to die.

Wortley was a scene of despair following the tragedy. The funerals were attended by thousands as, one after another, the funerals took place. A fund was set up to pay the burial costs and to erect a memorial to the children.

At the inquest there was criticism about the children's cotton-wool costumes, which was likened to being as dangerous as gunpowder. There were also recriminations against Eli Auty, who himself was badly burned about the hands whilst trying to extinguish the flames.

Cannon Brameld had been at St John's for only three months. He too, was criticised but declared he knew nothing about the Chinese Lanterns and he would have forbidden it if he had known. There was also disapproval that no one had seen the obvious danger from the previous evening's performance.

Although an 'Accidental Death' verdict was reached, it was declared that Cannon Brameld and Eli Auty had not exercised such forethought of care and supervision as had been their overall responsibility. There were, however, commendations for the way in which they had tried to save the children.

Cannon Brameld never really got over the tragedy.

One survivor, Sarah Kitchen, aged thirteen at the time of the fire, had been badly injured. She was required to go into hospital many times in the following years. Her sister, Maggie, had died in the fire. Later she married and became Sarah Hillman. Still disfigured by the fire, she had described in later years how, in the little room they had all been excited until one girl had upset her lantern and the falling candle had ignited her dress. In a few seconds there had been a mad scramble to get out of the room.

'I rushed to the only door to the street but it was locked. At the other doorway, leading to the school, was a platform which prevented us from escaping easily that way. As soon as help arrived and the door was unlocked, I rushed out, climbed a wall in the churchyard and in agony rolled in the thick snow between the gravestones.'

The memorial to the eleven children still remains in St John's Churchyard. There was the later addition of the name Alice Taylor on January 18th 1921, who died aged 42, 30 years after the tragedy. Alice's death was ascribed as being due to the fire on that dreadful night. Alice had suffered with the effects of the fire throughout her life, resulting in having both her arms amputated in 1920, the year before she died. The courageous Alice Taylor became the twelfth 'Snowflake' to die.

Colin Middleton

The Changing Face Of Batley

Batley, once a thriving town
From rags to riches came
Weaving cloth and carpets
For many a famous name

Rows and rows of houses
Standing back to back
Sharing outside toilets
Bathrooms they did lack

Five cinemas, a skating rink
Ballroom dancing too
Two swimming baths and pubs galore
Never lost for things to do

Our hospital's now a nursing home
Our cinema's out of town
We've only got one swimming bath
And our skating rink burned down

Even fish shops are changing
They're frying other things
Like sausages in batter
And spicy onion rings

Batley is a small town
With cobbled market place
While supermarket shopping
Sees its ever-changing face.

Beryl D Armitage

My Town ~ Then And Now

Industry once thrived in this Castleford town
Until the recession closed most of it down
Lumb's Glassworks, coke ovens, potteries and pits
'Nashcrete', now Hickson's, went down with the Blitz
Carrier bag and basket factories, tailoring and sewing
Small workplaces that helped the town in its growing
Shops were demolished to modernise the town
Even the Methodist Church was pulled down
Food shops like Redmans, Home & Colonial and Fishes
Gallon's, Melias, The Meadow weighed food to your wishes
The Globe, Farbers & Wheelers, Co-Op and Stein's
John P Wade, Mathews and Newboulds, all now has-beens
Phipps for fish, Sykes for tripe
Castleford & Alleton Stores, all the hype
Scarr's, Bellwoods, Pennington's, Rogers and Sweetings
Milners, Mercers, Ryan's, Ely's and Parkins
Fifty shilling tailors, Burtons, Blakes and Kendall's
Keaneys, Keyzers, Becketts and Rowalls
At the rear of the market, cheap meals could be bought
In a traditionally purpose-built 'British Restaurant'
Beer pulled with hand pumps was the order of the day
Delivered daily by horse and dray
Keel Inn, Miners, Wellington and Dragon
Red House, Railway, Queen's Head, Junction and Raglan
Star and Garter, Cock & Lion, the Crown
All these pubs have now been knocked down
Picture house, Albion, Star, Gaiety, the Queens
Rat Trap, cosy filmed the silver screens
Castleford Theatre Royal took centre stage
Entertaining families of any age
Kiosk, Parish Rooms, Albion, Co-Operative Hall
Dance halls where everyone had a ball
Florence Hall in summer was a swimming pool
In winter covered for dancing ~ real cool

Twice a year on 'Castlefields' the fair came to town
Now it is tarmaced and a car park laid down
Foam filled the streets from the River Aire
The market clock was a landmark for folk meeting there
The tram lines now have gone with the ark
On the old market place they have built a car park
We shop in the supermarkets, buy take-away grub
Bought from fast food outlets and the local pub
Night-clubs and bingo are the leisure attraction
You have to go elsewhere for a slice of the action
In our rugby team we still have pride
A new bus station when wanting a ride
Old people's homes have sprung up everywhere
And new doctors' surgeries for our health care
The jewel in the crown is 'Carlton Lanes'
A covered market and precinct to shop when it rains
An outside market open four days a week
Has put Castleford on the map so to speak
Let us give our young people some stimulation
To pass on to the next generation

Margaret Land

A Yorkshire Tyke

I'm proud to be a Tyke ~ Yorkshire through and through
Plain talking's what I like and living here's a joy.
Yorkshire pudding's a must when we eat
Sometimes for starters, at others with meat.

We've lots of tradition and come to the point
We're very outspoken and sometimes quite blunt.
We make good neighbours and welcome new folk
But don't stand for nonsense, life's not a big joke.

We're proud of our cricket, with lots of success
With Trueman and Hutton among the best.
At Elland Road their soccer's a treat
And shopping at Leeds is hard to beat.

At Haworth the Parsonage, full of culture
People queue to see its folklore.
The Bronte's wrote about the moors
Now people visit on their tours.

Ilkley's got a famous moor
A place to ramble, the air is pure.
A river flows right through the town
The 'cow and calf' are looking down.

We're short of nowt, we've everything here
With plenty of pubs all selling good beer.
Harry Ramsden's for fish and chips
A visit here is not to be missed.

So there you are and now you know
The places to see and where to go.
Just make a trip and see first hand
The finest county in the land.

Cow and Calf ~ Ilkley Moor

Harry Murtagh

Village Life

A few weeks ago I took part in a great event in the life of our community. It was the unveiling of a Wallhanging of Slaithwaite. I was very proud to have taken part in the stitching of it.

The idea started some years ago when some of the members of the Women's Institute, of which I am a member, saw a display at the Knitting and Stitching Show at Harrogate in 1997. Karima Ellis, of the local Moonraking event, did a sketch of the village and thought it would make a good starting point.

Without much hope, an application was filled in for an Art for Everyone Lottery Grant and in July 1997 a letter came to say we were successful. A plan began to take shape and meetings were held. Our group was only small, 18 or so. Karima was our artistic expert, Susan Fell, our organiser and Maureen Slingsby, our technical expert. Finally about 50 people took part, these included one man and one boy. Others helped in other ways, painting, joinery, making tea (lots of it) and other non-needlework jobs.

Stitching started in January 1998 and workshops were held weekly, first in the Community Centre then an empty Solicitor's office was offered to us. It was finally put together in the recreation room of the local Fire Station.

New crafts have been learned like felt making, stump work and needle-lace. A Calendar has been printed for 2001 showing part of the hanging, many of which will be sent worldwide.

The Wallhanging now hangs in the Community Centre. It measures approximately 8ft by 4ft. Two thirds of the panel represents the village, buildings in the centre and Hill Top and the fields beyond. The buildings are worked on canvas with the background sky, fields and trees in appliqué. The lower part depicts the life and happenings in the village, organisations, clubs, musical activities, textiles, industry, celebrations, sport, recreation and village services.

It has been a great community event and one of which we are all very proud, a work of art which will outlive us all.

Slaithwaite Wallhanging

Patricia Parkinson

By Worth

The Keighley coat of arms has a dragon,
A mythical beast,
Huge and powerful, breathing fire and smoke,
With hot breath that once,
Escaped through the forest of mill chimneys,
Now it may be found,
In industrial heat, glowing embers,
Inside the metal,
Sparks from the steel that strike against the stone,
That move through the pipes,
Heating systems and air conditioning,
It hisses inside,
With hard scales knocking against its prison,
Sometimes it escapes,
Lurks in the quiet streets but does no harm,
Undulating hills,
Hide the many coils of its fine barbed tail.
Its claws like tree roots,
Which nestle happily in the cool grass,
Till the dragon sleeps,
Hiding eyes as luminous as the moon,
Till he needs to wake.

Kathleen M Scatchard

16

Wakefield ~ What Might Have Been

I do not write so much about what Wakefield is or was,
But what it might have been.
Another *Beverley* or even *York* perhaps?
I wish the 'planners' could have seen
The desecration which they have bequeathed:
Cobblestones, bow windows, narrow streets, quaint shops ~
All gone.
'We must have progress, must move on!'

I doubt if we shall ever see again the likes of Sidebottoms and Scarrs
With baskets, tubs and brooms outside and nuts and bolts
Sold by the pound and served with pride.

The 'Bandwalk' near my home no longer echoes
To the sound of brass and drum
And Jerry Clay Lane china is no more.
The mansion house of Prophet Roe stills stands
And advocates communication of a different sort.
A few things stay the same ~ not everything has gone.
But what would our forefathers of yesteryear have thought ~
'We must have progress, must move on?'

Marjorie Holmes

Untitled

Alison Mace

Untitled

This is the Lodge belonging to Scarfe's Estate, Stanley, Wakefield.
The Lodge was the manager's home, a Mr A A Bond, seen here with bicycle.

The Manor House and Lodge are long gone, a council estate is there now. Some say Mr Scarfe used to haunt the grounds.

S Milner

Rescuing A Coat Of Arms

There's a piece of history
passed by one and all,
very few people notice it
because it's high up in the wall.

It's all that remains of a Public House
that once stood on this spot,
the trains still pass on Kirkgate Bridge
but the landscape's changed a lot.

My grandad worked for Crystal Spring,
he was Chief Engineer,
they bought the Pub and demolished it
later that same year.

The Coat of Arms was rescued
from the Public House remains,
restored to its former glory
once more positioned to watch the trains.

Crystal Spring has closed now
and my grandad's passed away.
He set it in the warehouse wall
and it remains there to this day.

Tim Wray

Hubris

When our factories were sold off quite quickly
thoughts of unemployment stalked us again
as drills and lathes stopped turning.
The quick-witted cockney football fans
waved wads of banknotes at us and chanted,
'You'll never work again,' in high good humour.

The great shining Thames Barrage protects them
from large sea surges that might occur
and yet could drown two million of them
(given deep depressions moving south with gales).
Even so we will not cheer to see them
floating slowly downstream with their banknotes.

J Sharratt

West Yorkshire

West Yorkshire has many faces:
Windswept moors and cobbled streets:
Harry Ramsden's famous fish 'n' chips,
Castle ~ abbeys ~ and country seats.

There's the peaceful Aire at Ilkley,
And its Cow and Calf rocks too.
You can walk up Beamsley Beacon
And enjoy a super view!

Our industries: based on wool and coal,
relied on our canals.
Now we're criss-crossed by motorways;
And our towns have shopping malls.

Mill chimneys are silent guardians,
Over houses built of stone.
The coal mines have been silenced.
Their last coal has been hewn.

Emley Moor mast points up to the sky,
Sculptures at Bretton Country Park,
Worth Valley Railway recalls the age of steam ~
The Alhambra ~ a beacon in the dark!

Chantry Chapel ~ built upon a bridge:
Bingley's Five Rise locks so high.
Halifax's 'Eureka' for children.
The Brontes, Howarth and moors nearby.

Yes! West Yorkshire has many faces!
In sunshine and in rain.
If you should visit West Yorkshire:
I'm sure you'll come again!

Nancy Webster

Royde's Mansion (The Hidden Jewel)

There's a mansion in middle of town
Royde's mansion, later Somerset House,
how sad it stands alone, forgotten.
A mystery to most Halifaxians.

How could such a magnitude of beauty
stay hidden from our eyes for so long,
shielded by mercantile and finance,
forgotten by the old, unknown by the young?

Where once ten young children played
chasing butterflies and picking flowers
in fields of green and skies of blue.
Can only be seen in our imagination.

Royde's love for his family was encased in plaster
to survive more than two hundred years.
Royde and spouse represented as Neptune and Britannia
their offspring an array of nymphs and medallions.

If this mansion could once again breathe
and its rooms come alive with sound
people would utter in sheer disbelief,
'There's a mansion in middle of town.'

J D Ashton

Castleford Town

On precinct benches old miners recline
Reflecting with sadness each closing mine
The decline of industry is tearing you down
Yes, times are a-changing for Castleford Town

You're losing your glass, confectionery and coal
It's breaking your heat, it's taking your soul
Your citizens are leaving, Smith, Jones and Brown
Yes, times are a-changing for Castleford Town

Our ancestors fought with strong Roman legions
They came to your bosom from far away regions
They wore helmets, cloth caps, but never a crown
Yes, times are a-changing in Castleford Town

Your chimneys are falling, your collieries shut down
The children unhappy, they weep and they frown
Tears swell your river, your streets they drown
Yes, times are a-changing in Castleford Town

They built you from coal, sweat and endeavour
They really believed it could go on forever
But now it's all fading, prestige, your renown
Yes, times are a-changing in Castleford Town

With inbred spirit move to Selby and Glories
And when the future tell grandchildren stories
They'll question, puzzle and ask with a frown
Tell me, 'Was there really a Castleford Town?'

Alan Town

24

Haworth

Dull, dark, grim and grey is Haworth in winter,
The cobbled street rises steeply, wet and shiny,
The stone cottages and shops that flank the hill
Convey an air of green dampness.
Such was the village the Brontes knew.
Surrounded by the lonely moor,
Imprisoned by the snow and fog,
Their fertile minds escaped into various fictions
And sought their freedom in fantasy.
But the summer brings visitors from near and far,
The hill is alive with adults and children.
But one cannot help but envisage,
The hardness, often cruelty of lives that are past,
Haworth in winter is an ever-present reminder.

E Wright

Memories Of My Childhood

Why is it that when we look back at our childhood all the days seemed to be sunny and carefree? My earliest recollection is living at No. 2 Sundial Terrace, Glen Lee, where I was born. All the lights seemed very strange to me, I learned in later years that the light shades had brown paper over them to dim the lights because my sister, Kathleen, had the measles and my parents were worried the light would damage her eyes.

My grandfather Ralph Thompson had a smallholding just down the road from where we lived and I spent many an hour there with him. He kept a pig, cows, calves, hens and a cockerel. The hen cote was in the farthest field and grandad would say come on, you can mix the hen, 'Jock' as he called it, it was mixed with water and had a lovely smell of bran. At hay-making time all the grandchildren played in the hayfield while our parents got on with the hay-making. All the days seemed to be sunny and warm. We would gather the hay into big rounds like a huge nest and then jump in. One of the things we all loved would be to be thrown up onto the top of the haystack and then slide down. We never tired of this. I remember feeling such peace and contentment. Lots of wild flowers grew in the field. I would gather milkmaids, buttercups, cowslips and make daisy chains.

On a Monday this was always washing day and in the kitchen was a mangle, peggy-tub and rubbing board. Grandad always managed to return from his smallholding in time to turn the handle for Grandma. The routine was all the whites went into the boiler then they were sorted, some went into dolly blue and some were starched. The washing had to be done in the day, dried, ironed and airing on the clothes horse by tea time. If it was raining the clothes were dried around a huge coal fire.

Because of all this activity Monday dinner had to be kept as simple to produce as possible. Cold beef from Sunday and Yorkshire pudding, warmed up, this had been made the day before in a big square tin and rose up the sides. I always hoped plenty would be left as this was my favourite way of eating it and gravy poured over which I have never tasted the like of since. 'Delicious'.

To say grandma was a good baker is probably to understate her. The most wonderful smells came from her kitchen. She made bread which I loved to knead, her own jams, raspberry, strawberry and damson, and the most wonderful ground rice tarts and coconut tarts. Kept on top of the kitchen cabinet was a butter churn and I would sometimes be allowed to help make the butter. We would take it in turns to turn the handle. The butter was then turned out onto a marble slab and patted into shape with wooden paddles.

My favourite tea was home-made bread and butter, damson jam and ground rice tart, all delicious. Sometimes soft cheese was available, called Demi Sel, lovely on brown bread.

Outside the back of my grandparents house was a yard and grandad had a hut there. In a child's eyes it seemed enormous but probably wasn't. In the hut he kept an incubator where he hatched out the chickens for his farm. When you went in it had a lovely smell of paraffin. It was lovely to see the chickens in various stages of growth, all fluffy and yellow. Grandad used lots of sawdust for his animals and I went with him to Whalleys timber merchants in Keighley for this. He had made a handcart and would use this for all kinds of things. When we got to Whalleys you had to go through the mill where all the big saws were. A trap door was in the floor and you went down into a kind of pit where all the sawdust collected from above. We filled the sacks and grandad threw them up through the trap door then he went up the ladder, reached down and pulled me up. I must at this time have been about three or four years. When the cart was loaded we started the long walk up to Glen Lee the cart must have felt very heavy for him.

Out the back of my grandparents house, when you passed through the yard gate, was a grassed area where all the washing was pegged out and at the bottom of this area was a very big wall to which a ladder was always leaning against. The wall was easily as tall as a house because in the corner stood a house called Delph Cottage whose roof at the back came down to some allotments where grandad had a plot of land. We would climb the ladder and go pick strawberries for grandma's jam. I don't think I was the best behaved of all the grandchildren because one day I decided it was very easy to climb on the roof of Delph Cottage and I sat dangling my legs over the edge. The others went to tell grandma and for my crime I was made to stay where she could see me at all times.

I suppose you could say there was nothing outstanding about Ralph and Paulina, just ordinary people going about their lives but times had not always been cosy. Ralph had come to Keighley about 1898. He was born at Appleton Le Moors and came looking for work. Here he married Ada Green and three little girls were born. To his sadness Ada died aged only 35 years and Ralph, with three very young children, re-married within the year. His second wife, Paulina Scott, was widowed and had a daughter, Lucy. They now had four daughters to raise between them. In 1914 Paulina gave birth to their son, also named Ralph, a much wanted and loved son.

In the following years Ralph's sister-in-law died leaving two children. The son stayed with his father but Ralph and Paulina added Mary to their brood and raised her as their own. The family were now five girls and one boy. Sadly, when the son Ralph Lowther, was eight he got an ear infection. He developed a mastoid which he had an operation for but the infection spread and he died. Ralph and Paulina were inconsolable.

My grandma Thompson must have been a very kind lady to raise her husband's three daughters and also his niece.

Lucy Adams

Think What He Must See

Of the statues that decorate the Town Hall, it's Mr
Cromwell that a sore thumb would relate to most
Of all.

There is his stonely shadow. He has stood there
Since before my time, and he'll be there after my
Next rhyme.

What a view it must be for Mr Oliver to see.

Traffic jams, which cause a pause. Pollution, which
Breaks through the O Zone doors.

A scuffle breaks out, but no Bobby about, to whistle
Law presence or stop the bout.

Think what else he must see.

Old people, young people, poor people, rich people.
Is it harmony?

Rich was our past in the mountains of wool, pumping
The mills till the sky became dull.

We were the centre of the world. Business boomed
As the sheep's coat was curled.

His vertical grave was placed up high, among a family
Of Royals stands this civilian guy.

Think what he must see.

Bees, trees, less government fees. Nature about its
Business and our kingdom peers in battle to rule us.

Some things never change. That's what I see.

Elliott Nash

Memories

I left school a few months before the start of WW2. I was 14 years old and I had two job offers: one on a farm at £1 a week, the other in a cotton mill at £1-1s a week. I went into the mill and enjoyed working there, even though the war was on with blackouts and rationing. As I remember it, everyone seemed to be happy at their work in those days. After working there for a year I was offered a job at James Clay and Sons Ltd Hollins Mill, with a promise of a 5s wage increase. I took it and stayed there until I was called up into the RAF in 1943.

These pictures were taken on Jan 26th 1961.

The building generating the heat was Hollins Mill, situated at the far end of Hollins Mill Lane, Sowerby Bridge. When it wasn't on fire it produced woollen cloth of the highest quality. In peacetime that went to make clothes for women; during WW2 it produced navy-blue for sailors, air-force-blue for airmen and hospital-blue for the wounded.

The morning after the fire. 300 people fearing for their jobs.

Basil Gibson

Yorkshire Pride

Chess in The Headrow, Leeds

S Orbaum

CLEVELAND

Church Street

A very small slice of social history

My acquaintance with Church street began when I was very young. It was war time. Dad was away in the army and mam worked as an early morning cleaner in some rather imposing offices just within screeching distance of the railway lines. Mam took me with her for a while because she was afraid to venture alone into the cavernous dark of the cellars where we filled monstrous coal buckets, one for every office plus bundles of sticks and rolled up newspapers. We worked as fast as we could, then mam hauled them up to the various offices. She set the fires, then swept, scrubbed and dusted while I polished the brass plates outside which proudly advertised 'Casper and Edgar' Shipping Agents.

These were hard times ~ harder on my mother than I realised. This was brought home to me one day with painful clarity.

It was early summer. Mam had changed her routine. With the lighter evenings we could go after school. It was good. On this particular day mam started cleaning out the grates while I went to the scullery for some brushes. Then I saw *it*. A crate, bulging with apples, the lid loosened and carelessly pushed to one side. I couldn't believe my eyes. I shouted for mam and we gazed with reverence at the creamy red apples, each one nestling in a frill of purple tissue. I imagined the taste. I had to. I couldn't remember if I had ever eaten one. Tentatively I reached out to touch them. 'Don't touch,' said my mother. The spell was broken. 'You leave them be.' I didn't argue and followed her around mooching and disconsolate until it was time to leave. We closed the office doors and returned to the scullery to dispense with our brushes and cloths. Slowly and deliberately mam took off her pinny and enclosed it in her brown paper carrier. We moved towards the door. Mam looked back. 'B***** it!' she said, and quick as a flash scooped three apples and pushed them down into her bag, her face red and frightened. Together we stepped outside.

Hundreds of women streamed from the shipyards in the fading sunlight. They marched proudly in their boots and bib and brace overalls ~ three and four abreast. Each wearing a turban with windsweeps of hair tied up on top.

We joined their procession up Church Street. Mam grimly determined. Me, deliriously happy, I had three apples, one for me, and one for each of my sisters.

The women chattered. Mam knew one or two and gradually joined in their repartee. Eventually she relaxed and I heard her confess. 'I've just pinched three apples for me bairns.' The women squealed and shouted approval. One of them nodded at me saying, 'You'll be all right then,' and I was. Oh yes, I was all right.

Pat McKenna

Growing Up In The 50s And 60s ~ (West) Hartlepool

We who grew up in the 40s and 50s of what was then West Hartlepool were, on the whole, healthy, happy and contented children. Our parents had no car or TV, our homes had only coal fires and we only usually got toys bought for us at Christmas and on our birthdays. New clothes were a necessity only when we had outgrown something, but there was a lot of passing down within families. Easter, however, was one time when you got new shoes and socks if nothing else. Most mothers knitted and sewed for their children and generally made do and mended.

Confined to the house after dark or during bad weather, we always found plenty to do. If you were lucky, you had a doll's house or toy shop or a small desk and blackboard. There were jigsaws and board games and books to read and colour. While you played, you listened to the radio ~ music, comedy shows, variety, serials, quiz shows and plays. It was usually too cold to play in the bedroom, so you played under the watchful eyes of your parents and did not mind at all.

Our back street in Studley Road was always clean and tidy, thanks mostly to each family keeping their own 'patch' dirt and litter free. Everyone used their back door when they went out, so there was always someone to keep an eye on the children playing there with bats and balls, skipping ropes, skates and, for some lucky ones, bicycles. Children of all ages 'played out' and older children watched out for the younger ones. There was little fighting or bullying and certainly no stone throwing.

Older children were allowed to go further afield and two streets away led to the steelworks bridge and the beach. We took no food and did not need a towel because we did not go into the sea. We played unmolested for hours and returned home when we felt hungry or the weather turned inclement.

In the other direction and across a busy road were the Burn Valley gardens where we played on the swings and slide or the rockery, looked for tiddlers in the lily pond or skated endlessly round and round the bandstand that used to be there. There was so little traffic that you could go and return wearing your skates. I cannot remember any child being injured by a motor vehicle in our area, even though once you could ride a two-wheeler bike you went on the road.

Saturday mornings we went to the Picture House club where we saw feature length films, cartoons and a serial and sometimes had a sing-song or concert given by other children. When it was your birthday you could sit upstairs and take a friend free.

Sunday afternoons meant Sunday School and then very often a walk with your parents and siblings, to the park or Seaton Carew, everyone dressed in their best. Even on a wet or very cold Sunday you did not mind being taken to the museum as there always seemed to be something new to discover or old favourites to see.

We were allowed to go 'down town' on Saturday afternoons and during school holidays to spend some or all of our pocket money, usually on sweets and comics or trinkets. Girls always seemed to buy note books and pencils, hair slides and 'jewellery'.

As well as regular trips to the cinema with your parents, you always made a point of going to the Hartlepool carnival's parade and showground. There was a pantomime on at the Empire every Christmas, as well as those put on by the dancing schools. Occasionally there was a visiting circus or fair.

With no money for holidays or other luxuries, we got our enjoyment fairly close to home all year and every year, but what a wealth of memories we all have ~ ask anyone who is now in their 50s or 60s.

Enid Allen

Redcar Town

Propelling Hinton's shopping trolley's across grey tarmac car parks, legs kicking, near the telephone exchange, aged 8½.
Dirty, litter-strewn back alleys behind my childhood home in Red Lion Street.
Collecting beer-bottle tops at the Navy Club and returning Lowcock's fizzy pop bottles for the deposits.
Cowboys and Indians on the wasteland between the Co-Op dairy and Central Motors Garage, potash trains hurtling past under a rickety footbridge.
Launching firework rockets along the lengthy station platform on November 5th, or thereabouts.

In wintertime, freak waves crash against concrete sea walls, inadequate from their conception, flooding the amusement arcades.
Police barriers seal off the seafront promenade, cold North Sea winds of Arctic origin penetrate your cloth defences, freezing to the bone.
Half-knackered red buses pass by, inches away from the bag-laden shoppers, past Frankie Dee's, the Red Lion Pub ~ before pedestrianisation.
While British Steel puffs carbon brown clouds of dust into the sky, hazy and surreal.

Steel Galas, Donkey Derbies, motor boats in the Coatham Enclosure.
The wail of illuminated skeletons in the Ghost Train at Cadona's Amusement Park.
Children building dens on windswept sand-dunes, metal detector enthusiasts fanning away furiously for anything both metallic and precious.
Part-lame, careworn donkeys, trot without sincerity of intent, their child passengers cajoling and laughing, a time before our animal rights issues.
The TransExpress hums its motorised way to and fro, tractor tracks in the sand.

Busy horse-racing days, as now, menfolk roaming from pub to pub, comparing tips, cards and forecasts.
Before heading for the sacred turf, bleary-eyed and speculative.

While the women shop, dragging bored stubborn offspring, faces contorted, through the crowds.

(Before the arrival of the 'Golden Arches'.)

To the council estates uniformity of poverty, of the Closes or West Dormanstown.

Before the oppressive backdrop of the ICI plant, now 30 or more different companies.

Redcar-by-the-Sea, bypassed by investors, soon I'll be saying goodbye, my memories buried by Morrisons and the Wilton Street Shopping Development.

Dean Thomas Axford

A Cleveland Traverse

The Lyke Wake walk
sets many to talk,
whilst the White Rose Way
should be walked in May.

High on Roseberry Topping
there is much rock outcropping,
and the Cleveland Way
needs more than a day.

Now whilst out hiking,
remember some are biking.
But, the Australian G'day
can be heard down Whitby way.

Going on to Billingham Beck
you are on to a Heritage trek,
follow into Hartlepool of old,
renowned and Monastically told.

A daughter, St Hilda, of a Northumbrian thane,
taught Christianity at Heretu, by name,
with Anglo-Saxon monks and nuns,
lived and prayed, where the North Sea runs.

So with a fast gait and fare,
start at the Sandwell gate and chare,
proceed with your Holy quest
and visit as St Hilda's guest.

Alan Noble

Which Way To Middlesbrough?

Middlesbrough, seems to be
Missing from road signs, so you see
Visitors, coming to our town
Permanently, wear a frown
It's so hard for them to know
Just which way, they should go
From the A1, the A168 we take
Then A19, don't make a mistake
After that, a big mystery
Which road to turn off, seems to be
A dilemma, for strangers, here
Thornaby, Acklam, it was where
We came off for the theatre, at Middlesbro'
How would strangers know, to go
They would carry on the way
To County Durham, before they
Found that they'd missed Middlesbro'
So, we do really know
Better signs, should be in place
To tell folks which way to face
To find the fine town, that we have here
Which, to us, is so very dear

Joyce Metcalfe

Home

I live in a small town, but it's big-hearted,
Only known for iron and ore when it first started.
Now there's more to us there is,
Big buildings and well-known businesses!

There's many sights you can see,
Like Dorman's museum for history.
Roseberry Topping you can climb,
See Captain Cook's museum, go back in time!

If you like blue sky and plenty of greenery,
Visit Albert or Stewarts park for great scenery.
Enjoy the nightlife, dance at the Venue,
Eat at our restaurants, check out the menu!

'Come on the *Boro*' we shout out loud,
Through the good and bad we stand proud.
Wearing our shirts, heads held high,
We've got the best team, that's not a lie!

All sorts of people live here with me,
Babies, youth, people old as can be.
Now let's not forget those brave that died,
Honoured with a monument, we look at with pride!

We may one day leave and wander,
Uproot the North-East and go yonder.
Even visit the South-place with the Dome,
But one thing's for certain,
    We'll Always Say 'Boro's Our Home'!

Pahani Kaur

The Zetland Lifeboat

The sea is alive, she has a heart and soul.
Many lives she has taken in the days of old.
Scars are scattered far out to sea.
Wrecks of ships that used to be.

The Zetland Lifeboat, she still lives one.
Too old to work, her oars now gone.
Retired to her graveyard in a museum to show,
How many lives she saved so long ago.

Replaced by an engine, all modern and new.
Yet she still looks after the fishermen, now few.
She has the same name, but now she's moved on.
She's faster, better but not as strong.

Her strength was in the men who rowed her to sea.
Crashing through the waves,
She was an awesome sight,
Heaving, heavily deep into the night.

Searching for lost souls at sea.
Looking as far as the eye can see.
Watching the horizon until night becomes day.
Echoes of voices from far away.

Replaced by an engine, all modern and new.
Yet still she returns when called.
She returns to the sea with heart so strong,
Where sailors still shout and echo their song.

Andrew Brian Zipfell

Saltburn Sands

Sandy beach stretches for miles
Fringed by a grey placid sea.
Gentle waves tickle the shore;
In the sky, seagulls fly free.

High Hunt Cliff touched by the sun
Shadows black rocks far below,
Where children search in the pools,
And parents walk to and fro.

Fishermen stand on the pier
And cast their lines from the side.
Whilst ships on the skyline wait
For the turning of the tide.

Pillars of steam from the works
Lazily rise to the sky.
An aeroplane leaves a trail
As it flies a course nearby.

Tiny birds dance on the shore
And leave their tracks in the sand.
Passers-by smile in delight
At their antics on the strand.

At Saltburn the sun shines bright
On this special New Year's Day.
Welcomes the millennium
To this sandy cliff bound bay.

Huntcliff, Saltburn

Wendy Castling

Cleveland's Eston Hills

Eston Hills in Cleveland are situated in our heavy industrial area, with ICI Chemicals and British Steel practically at the foot of them, which makes us appreciate the hills very much. We can look past smoking chimneys and see the hills in their seasonal ever-changing colours, covered in snow or their peaks shrouded in mist. We can see the sun rise above them and the moon sink behind them and at dusk they appear very mysterious. A stark contrast to the brilliant illuminations of ICI nearby.

Centuries of people in Cleveland have enjoyed the sight of Eston Hills and generations have enjoyed climbing and rambling on them. There are not many local kids who have not climbed to the top or spent happy hours picking bilberries, brambles and bluebells on the slopes. Purple lips, grazed knees and rosy cheeks are legacies of a day spent on the hills. Eston Nab is the highest point ~ 242 metres above sea level ~ and it is well worth the climb up the well-worn paths for the views. On clear days we can see over the haze of industry and urban development to the sea and far horizons.

Eston Nab has always been a vantage point in wars for the observation of enemy invasion and excavations suggest that defended enclosures were built on The Nab as early as 700BC. During the Napoleonic wars with France, a sandstone beacon was constructed and a small cottage nearby, and in the second world war the Home Guard manned the site against invasion from the air. The sandstone buildings were demolished in 1956 and a stone pillar now marks the site of Eston Nab.

When ironstone was discovered in Eston Hills mining began in 1850 by Bolckow and Vaughan and the hills at Eston became a hive of industry. Then a railway was built to transport the ironstone and sandstone cottages built for the miners. These cottages, close to the foot of the hills and mines railway, are there to this day, and the people who lived and worked there have spoken of those times with nostalgia, recalling a close-knit community in spite of the hardships endured.

The miners have been aptly named 'Men of Iron' and a video has been made about them. Their work was gruelling, dangerous and dirty ~ what a transformation it must have been for them to emerge from the depths of the mine to the natural beauty of Eston Hills, mining ceased in 1949 after almost a century of excavating ironstone.

Before motoring and travelling became so popular people walked more and local people walked mostly up Eston Hills. A Social History of days gone by was written by a local man, M E Wilson, entitled 'The Story of Eston'. He wrote that:

> 'Eston Hills was a popular mecca in fine weather with families tramping up from South Bank and Grangetown (which were small towns with rows of street houses built for steelworkers and ship builders). They took the air and admired the view, with youngsters playing in the bracken and heather, and adolescents doing a spot of spooning in the gorse. And on Bank Holidays crowded trains from Middlesbrough discharged their noisy cargoes to wend their way up the hills, and there to climb and puff, or sit and dream as the younger ones skipped or played football or cricket on the green. The banks were alive with fun and games, while man and his mate relaxed from arduous toil.'

Climbing hills is thirsty work and when I was a kid in the thirties we used to take bottles of water to drink, but a Granny Miller reputedly sold water, drawn from a well, for a halfpenny a glass to thirsty holidaymakers. As there were literally thousands of people on the banks, her sandstone cottage at the bottom of a quarry on the hills, was ideally situated. Today, a motorway has been built along the foot of Eston Hills, and also houses, but the hills themselves remain mostly the same. They have been there for the stone age people, Romans, Saxons, Edwardians, Victorians, and for us, and will surely be there for future generations.

In a changing world we can still ramble and climb on them, pick bilberries in summer and sledge down them in winter. If we need fresh air and exercise, solitude or solace, they are there. When we are tired of the sights, smells and noise of industry Eston Hills can restore our jaded senses.

Olga King

Did You See Them?

There was a lion in Middlesbrough!
Fierce of mien, but eyes of woe,
And birds . . . scary . . . Huge-claws.
Exhausted foxes. Stuffed of course!
We went to see 'em,
In the Albert Museum,
Years ago.

Stella Varey

Cyclo-Cross, South Bank, January 1998

Klaxon sounding, heart pounding
Hands gripping, wheels slipping
Grass thinning, pedals spinning
Hill steepening, mud deepening
Legs quaking, mud caking
Crowd funning, feet running
'Only one hour to go!'
And then it starts to snow . . .

Bob Goodall

Life In Middlesbrough

What do you see as you wander around, derelict buildings in parts of
our town.
Streets littered with rubbish, coke cans and the like, youths on the
pavements, riding their bikes.
Dogs without owners left freely to roam, fouling the footpaths,
running on roads.
On the street corners the young are in mobs, hanging around without
any jobs.
But life in this town isn't all doom and gloom, with shopping malls
and walkways, there's plenty of room.
Cafes and restaurants, with good food to eat, a nice cosy bus station
with plenty of seats.
Delightful flower beds, a joy to behold, beautiful parks to suit young
or old.
Museums, Art Galleries, Nature Trails and more, Cinemas,
Bingo Halls and Pubs galore.
A short ride on a bus you reach country or coast, beautiful scenery of
that we can boast.
The majority of teenagers studying so hard, to improve the image
with which they are tarred.
Trying to show that they are not all the same, it's only the minority
who put us to shame.
The folk are so kindly, always willing to help ~ if you visit
Middlesbrough, you'll see for yourself.

Cathleen Thomas

The Seacoal Gatherers

On the beach at Seaton Carew
So many flocked, it was the life that we knew,
Overshadowed by darkness, in the middle of the night
Gathering seacoal, working only by moonlight,
Skinny kids muffled up against the bitter gale
Collecting the shiny black treasure, spilling over their pails,
Young and old raking the coal, icy water teeming into their wellies
To cook the food to fill their hungry bellies,
Seacoal bags, crammed so tight
Would set the fire blazing bright,
Orange flames licking, heating the old black oven
Where fresh bread baked and sometimes a rice pudding,
Yet even though times were very hard
If we had a seacoal pile stocked in the yard,
We had smiles on our faces, that was for sure
Although we were working class folk and really quite poor.

Vannesa Fitzgerald

West Hartlepool

I remember the picture house and the Regal
The Northerns, the Gaiety, the Lex
The Majestic, the West Ends, the Forum
The Empire, with none showing sex

We had a matchbox factory
Robinson's and Woolworth's store
A milk dairy in Villiers Street
Plus quite a lot more

We had the Queen's Rink for dancing
The steelworks were doing well
Shipyards, full and working
What more can we tell?

Horse-drawn carts for everything
Delivering milk, coal and such
Even the rag and bone man
Seemed to give so much

Brushes hard, brushes soft
To keep our houses clean
No such thing as a Hoover
Or a washing machine

Seacoal on the fire
No tele or telephone
Smoke billowing everywhere
We had no smokeless zone

We had patches on our trousers
No socks on our feet
Countryside walks and rambles
Were classed as a treat

Over the years quite a lot has gone
Just one picture hall in sight
One day they may all come back
I can only hope I'm right.

George E Bage

Untitled

If I picked a place to live, it has got to be right here,
No other place could be as good, I hold it very dear.
I have seen the changes thick and fast
All sailed on into the past.
I have always longed, for faraway places,
Of different towns and different races.
But as I have aged, I have settled back,
Motivation, I now lack.
I am planted here, my roots have grown,
No other place could I call home.
With Jackson's Landing and the Marina's Bay,
I finally think we are paving the way.
I am glad I stayed and did not roam.
This town is great, I call it home.
To take my pick, I am no fool,
The place that is best is Hartlepool.

B Tyers

COUNTY DURHAM

Memories Of Our Steamy Days

Historic modes of transport have always held a strange fascination for me, even from childhood, therefore, coming from the North East of England, the birthplace of the railway, it isn't surprising that trains should be included, especially the steam trains.

As a child in the early 1950s, I was often seen with my cousins and friends, standing on the bridge, overlooking the railway track at Shildon station. We were waiting patiently for one of those vast steam locomotives to come chugging in so that we could take note of their engine numbers, then we would run home, our faces black with the smoke from the steam funnels.

An extra special treat was to see The Flying Scotsman come through our station. What a thrill! You could hear its whistle blowing a mile down the track and when it came into view, I can't describe the wonder of seeing that big black engine with its bright gold name plate. It was definitely the king of the steam trains.

Shildon was the home of the Wagon Works, built in 1832 specifically for the making and repairing of the freight train wagons and their various parts. Two of my uncles worked there and it was known as Shildon Shops.

Timothy Hackworth was a well-known name in Shildon. He was one of the first engineers to be identified with the creation of the Stockton to Darlington Railway. Hackworth also had a school named after him where I attended from the age of 5 until, at the age of 9½, I left to move to Darlington with my parents.

At Darlington's Bank Top Station I used to love to see George Stephenson's Locomotive No.1 standing proudly on the platform, reminding people that it was the first train to run on the first railway track. It now stands in the North Road Railway Museum which used to be Darlington's only railway station.

In the 1960s some brand new, shiny diesel trains were introduced and would take us for rides to nearby seaside towns of Redcar and Saltburn but I always preferred the steam trains. Summer holidays were made more exciting by the thrill of our journey on a steam train. When the whistle blew it meant we were approaching a tunnel and we would sit, rigid with terror as everything went black. My dad would pull on the leather strap to close the carriage window before

56

the train entered the tunnel because all the dust and smoke would blow back into the carriages. When we heard the whistle again we knew we'd soon see daylight and laugh with relief. It was scary but fun!

Now we look back on those majestic modes of transport as being creators of pollution but in the days when we stood on the platform, in awe of the big shiny engines with their bright gold name plates and saw them chugging in and out of the station, whistle blowing and great gushes of black smoke billowing high into the air, we were so full of admiration that the idea of ecological disaster didn't enter our minds.

On the A66, just outside Darlington, on land formerly recognised as being part of the original Stockton-Darlington track, stands a brick sculpture of a train. It was commissioned by Darlington Borough Council and a local supermarket and supported by Northern Arts. The designer was David Mach and the train contains 181,754 bricks.

In the town centre, on High Row, is a floral model of the Locomotive No.1. We are proud of our railway heritage in Darlington.

This Sculpture contains 181,754 bricks

The Brick Train Sculpture standing on the A66 ring road into Darlington.

Margaret S Browne

57

The Club Trip

Once upon a time, folk in this area could boast
About how clean the beaches were along our North East coast.
Redcar, Saltburn, Whitby, were noted for their sand
Where one could lie quite comfortably in a quest to get sun-tanned.
We used to go to Redcar, twice a year in fact,
And we got so excited on seeing the bags being packed
With sandwiches and sausage rolls, hard-boiled eggs and pop,
Swimming gear and sand shoes and a towel on the top.

Trips were run for members' kids of the workmen's clubs,
And all of them got five bob each from the yearly subs
To spend on what we wanted and how we smacked our lips
At the thought of eating candy floss, rock and bags of chips.
And the weather never bothered us, as come rain or shine
The buses that were chartered took us to the sand and brine.
I've seen us sit in tents all day because it's poured with rain,
But I've also seen folk blistered as in the sun they've lain.

At 12 o'clock precisely the sands saw a transition,
As not a man was to be seen, for keeping with tradition,
They'd seen their wives and kids alright with deck chairs and a tent
And said to them, 'We'll see you soon,' and off to the club they went.
Soon after all the men had gone it was time to eat our lunch
And often with the boiled egg some shell and sand we'd munch,
But it didn't harm us as the sand was always clean
As there'd been no dirty dogs around using it as a latrine.

The younger kids played happily with a bucket and spade
Or ruined all the sand castles the older ones had made.
And then the cry went up, 'That's it, I'll not make any more,
I'm off down to the water to see what's been washed ashore.'
If the day was warm enough we'd play happily in the sea,
But the hardiest amongst us would swim regardlessly.
I've seen them come out shivering ~ lips blue with the cold
And their mothers saying to them, 'That'll teach you to be bold.'

By half past two to three o'clock the scene changed once again,
As the menfolk, fed and watered, returned to entertain
Their lively sons and daughters so the mothers now could go
And have a decent cup of tea and a game of prize bingo.
Then they'd stretch their legs a bit with a walk along the front
And maybe pop into a gift shop where for a bargain they would hunt.
They left their favourite until last ~ a knickerbocker glory,
Then stroll back to the sands again, feeling hunky-dory.

Not long after they came back, it was time for us to leave
And we'd return the tent and deck chairs, the deposits to retrieve.
Then, if we were lucky, on our way back to the bus,
We could spend it in the amusement park,
Rounding a great day off for us.

Joyce Crawford

From Conception To Millennium

This is the story of Stephenson, and Hackworth
Midwives in attendance at the railway's birth
Locomotion and Rocket, enshrouded in steam,
Darlington to Stockton, the 'Ultimate Dream'.
Crowds cheered, a man with a red flag in the lead,
The first Iron Horse, 8 miles an hour, the average speed.

The track, rampant, sweeping far, worldwide,
Bridging rivers, valleys, through mountainsides.
Small trains, carrying Victorians to the coast
For cream-teas, and dainty triangles of toast.
Huge engines, wheels shouting clickety clack,
Glowing fires, trailing smoke from their stack.

Diesel, Electric, fast, sleek and clean,
Replaced the dirty, noisy, but romantic steam.
Electrification, the 125, and jointless track,
Tilting trains that hum, no clickety clack.
Stephenson and Hackworth, benevolently sight,
Look down, chests out, proud heads held high.

C Matthews

NORTHUMBERLAND

Warkworth

Slate grey fortress.
Battle scarred and weary,
Warrior no longer,
Abandoned to your fate.

Strategically vital,
Defender of the North,
Once the pennants of the Percy's,
Flew from your gates.

Earls of Northumberland.
Their crests set in stone,
Proclaimed authority and ownership,
Made you home.

Invasion and battle,
Endured with equal calm,
Stalwart as a sentinel,
Three hundred years of storms.

The lions then departed,
Picked Warkworth to the bone,
Deserted, left to nature,
For a rescuer to come.

Empty arched windows,
Stare out across the sea,
Await their restoration,
Renew their history.

In spring a million daffodils
Swaying beneath your walls,
Delighted visitors, in plenty,
Gaze on a yellow sea of hope.

Moya Charlton

Untitled

Tenantry Column and War Memorial, Alnwick

Anne L Hopper

Lindisfarne

With grubby fingers
across the map we traced
their holy snail-trails
Columba and Cuthbert
and Aidan the gentle,
who, ferrying Christ's word
through turbulent waters
in currachs, frail as
spinning leaves in Autumn,
choose their rocky spaces ~
places between dark waves
and golden heaven
where wild birds winged and wailed
and called like souls in need
of praying and shriving.

Here, I walk on stones
that once knew Aidan's
humble feet. I hear a wind
keen softly, through rough grasses,
mourning the lost.

This is the Holy Island
of saints, of scholars ~
sanctified, long since,
by Columba and Cuthbert
and Aidan the gentle.

Áine Máire Chadwick

TYNE & WEAR

Riverside Café

They were not what I expected to see
When I leaned from the small rear window:
I could feel my face contort with revulsion.
Rats . . . loathsome! I shivered yet watched ~
Quick, lively, busy, concentrated, unlovely,
Scurrying from the water, across the muddy clay
To the tunnelled architecture they had crafted.
All around them, the beauty that draws the tourists ~
The placid river, the steep wooded cliff
With its enclaves of primrose, bluebell and
Wild garlic; surmounting all, the splendour
Of cathedral and castle: historic Durham.
And at the base of all the grandeur ~ this,
This scuttling life: wet fur, spiked and dripping,
Eyes wary and guarded.

I thought of cholera and bubonic plague . . . and Hitler
Ugly with hatred, screaming for the death of Jewish rats,
Knowing that human instinct says 'Kill' . . . And yet
They bring us death as innocently as the bee
Gives honey. And if I were jailed and solitary
Behind this window, I would learn to welcome
Their companionship. Familiarity breeds affection.

I asked myself, 'Why?'
Why am I watching rats at the water's edge?
Why not straining up to view the sky-sloped
Towers? But to avert the eyes is to falsify
Experience, distort some facets of the truth.
There is beauty and aesthetic pleasure, yes,
But there are the poor forked creatures of
Lear's vision who must accommodate their lives
To hunger, squalor, and the daily ministry of rats.

My friend in the tea-room barely noticed my return.
'Isn't it a truly magnificent view?' she said.
'I'm glad we came.'

Durham Cathedral on the River Wear

Alice Fairclough

The Talk Of The Town

Details of this elopement, recorded in a book relating to the history of Newcastle, inspired me to relate them, in my own way, via the poem.

A wealthy Newcastle merchant
Mr Aubone Curtees, by name
In seventeen seventy-two
By his daughter Bessie, was shamed

When she, eloped with a houseman
Her lover, a man named John Scott
Though in time, it was broadly felt
That quite a good catch, Bessie got!

From an upstairs window she left
With her lover, helping her down
Via a ladder, he'd placed there
They became, the talk of the town!

John later, became Lord Eldon
When of course, in stature he grew
Enough it seems to warrant more
And was made, Lord Chancellor too!

The very house, Bessie lived in
Still stands, on the way to the Quay
Where visitors, even today
On hearing this tale, flock to see

Who would have thought, the gossip
Would thrive, over two centuries
And keep alive the story
Of John Scott, and Bessie Surtees?

Patricia Whittle

The Stadium Of Light

There is a new football ground, called the Stadium Of Light,
When you pass it, it stands out bright,
As it stands on the old Wearmouth Colliery site.
Since it was built, the number of fans have soared,
All of them have chanted and roared.
The ball has hit the net,
The game is not over yet.
The striker has scored a goal,
Now he is running around the pitch like a new-born foal.
The fans are shouting for more,
And asking what is the score?
Sunderland are in the lead,
As the striker has used his heed.
The Stadium Of Light replaces the old Roker Roar
That stands at Roker no more.

Tina Rooney

Gateshead ~ An Evolutionary Tale

Anyone over fifty years old, with connections with the Sunderland Road area of our town, will well remember the dingy passageway which once served as the grand entrance to the Old Fold estate from Emily Street under the railway line there. How the water dripped down the inside walls, and how pedestrians ran the risk of having their clothes smeared by the muck should they meet a pram coming in the opposite direction whilst passing under the bridge!

They will also remember the tall railway sleepers at the top of Old Fold Road, opposite Cross Row, which surrounded the allotment gardens, and the prefabricated buildings opposite which, at various times, housed a library (1941), a children's clinic, and a nursery school. They will recall the enormous field which was the Clarke-Chapman football pitches, and the little park tucked away in the corner, with its swings, and slide, and teapot lid roundabout.

People of the town will remember the old Sunderland Road library built in 1934 behind the Palace (Old Blacks) cinema, the 'hikey park', which is still there, of course, and the old Sunderland Road school.

It is fascinating to examine the old minutes of meetings which represent the machinery of Gateshead council, and to understand how the politicians of the town have shaped the recent history of the above sites, linking them in a way which they never anticipated.

The allotment gardens fell into misuse many years ago and, as the number of railway sleepers dwindled, shortcuts were established across the land. In the 1970s the Old Fold Community Centre was established there after a long battle for community facilities for the estate.

Simultaneously, but connected, plans were set in motion to replace the old Sunderland Road branch library. Councillors earmarked a possible site where the school had been demolished and another, at the foot of Herbert Street, was seen as a likely site. The latter site on the hikey park proved to be a stumbling block for the Council, however, because the land was originally leased by the Council (to be precise, the Mayor, Aldermen and Burgesses of the Borough of Gateshead) from the Master and Ancient Brethren of the Hospital of King James Hospital at the princely sum of £64.54 per year until the year 2103, and it has a restrictive covenant restricting its use; during the period of the lease the land is to be used only 'as a recreation ground for the free use of the inhabitants of the Borough of Gateshead'.

With that in mind, the Library, Arts and Shipley Gallery Committee resolved that the decision to site the replacement library at Herbert Street should be rescinded.

The Council persisted with the negotiations with the owners of the land, and early in 1978 it was announced that agreement had been reached regarding the variation of the covenant covering the hikey park site, and as compensation for using part of the land for the new library it was announced that the way was open for the Policy and Resources Committee to appropriate land at Cross Row, for the sum of £4270, financed under the Inner Cities Partnership Construction Package.

The new library was officially opened on 11th June 1979, and opened to the public from 1pm that day.

On the land appropriated as compensation, a children's park was prepared at Cross Row. It seemed to serve the community well ~ for a time ~ until it fell into disrepair through vandalism, and all the equipment was removed.

Unfortunately that land did not have imposed upon it the same restriction that it could only be used for recreational purposes ~ an oversight at the time, perhaps, but in recent years the Old Fold Community Centre has been removed also, and the land is now being used to build new bungalows to provide housing for the aged.

The old library/clinic/nursery at Old Fold Road has long gone, replaced by the Bede Community School, and a new community park has been developed close by.

History is turning full circle, as the history of Gateshead evolves.

Bill Pickard

Death Of The River Tyne

Such is life ~ once full of care
We now *have* time to stand and stare,
Across the Tyne, with waters deep,
So quiet now ~ almost asleep.

Once ~ full of life ~ it is no more,
So sad ~ the Tyne has closed its door
To sounds of shipyards in full swing,
Where every trade ~ just ~ did their thing.

When skills of men were put to test,
'Twas no great feat ~ they were the best.
It is so sad from that great quest
Those skills will now be ~ laid to rest.

Expertly built from keel to crest,
They sailed the world from east to west.
Those floating monuments of steel,
With noble seamen at the wheel.

They sailed on time ~ they looked so fine,
A credit to their shipping line,
The end of an era ~ it is a crime,
For great ~ shipbuilding ~ on ~ *The Tyne*.

Norman H McGlasham
South Shields

Coals To Newcastle

Coals ti Newcastle the sayin used ti be,
Just a kind iv joke that was there for aall ti see.
Wi' coal mines aall aroond us, scattered far and near,
Scarred by mucky slag heaps and flagged by windin' gear,
It wornt as if wi had a say in what wi thowt iv it,
It was just a way iv life ~ and life went on aroond the pit.

We looked doon on Waallsend from the Coast Road in them days
Clouded from the sun by the soot and smoke-filled haze.
We nivor thowt it strange ~ that was how it had ti be
Ti keep wa hooses waarm, you'd want a fire on you see.
And fires needed coal, and coal yi must admit
Was only ti be fund, if men went doon the pit.

Some didn't want ti gan, but how could the' refuse
Tha wasn't many options, you couldn't pick and choose.
At fowerteen there was nowt else, they had ti orn tha keep;
For dad and Uncle Tom, pride was dear and labour cheap.
It was just the way things wor and they made the best iv it,
Like tha fathers and tha brothers, who were also doon the pit.

But noo tha's nee coal fires; the time has come to pass
Where every hoose is 'lectric, and the heatin' comes from gas.
Them who woarked as miners ended signin' on the dole
And tha's bairns today who've nivor even seen a bit iv coal.
'Coals ti Newcastle!' ~ we'll see the likes iv it
'Cos tha isn't any left ~ and we haven't got a pit.

Neebody imagined that one day they would close,
Noo, yi nivor see a pit ~ wouldn't want tee ah suppose,
Where once the coll'ry windin' gear and pit heed baths both stood
Tha's just a grassy mound and trees ~ the rest is gone for good.
With luck it's ganna stay that way, it's neither reet nor fit
That men should hev to sweat and toil for coal doon in the pit.

Bob Proud

Howay The Lads!
(Apologies to G K Chesterton)

Before the Spartans came to Blyth, or Magpies were full grow'd,
The little Geordie drunkard made the famous Scotswood Road.
A rambling road, a shambling road, that wanders up and down
And after him the polis ran, the bailiff, half the town.
A busy road, a boozy road, where we did drink our fill
The night we went to Gallowgate ~ by way of Rowlands Gill.

I have no truck with bailiffs, I've never thumped a copper,
And if I took on half the town I'd come a right old cropper.
But I would bash their heids in if they came all array'd
To straighten out the crooked road the drunken Geordie made.
Where you would see wor lad and me, with broon ale in our hands
The night we went to James's Park ~ by way of Tynemouth Sands.

His sins were all forgiven him, or why do boozers thrive
To gan alang the Scotswood Road, like when he was alive?
He staggered forth from left to right and knew not which was which
But the Blue Star shone above him when they found him in the ditch.
So glare at us, or swear at us, we did not see so clear
The night we went to Roker Park ~ by way of South Shields pier.

My friends, we may not go again to see the Blaydon Races
And all the lads and lasses with their bright and smiling faces
But I will walk beside you to St James's Leazes end
And we will shout, 'Howay the lads, Newcassel's won agen!'
For there are cup ties to be played, and finals to be seen
Before we go to Paradise ~ by way of Jesmond Dene.

Evelyn Barnett

Castletown Carol

When the grass was pale and silvery
Shimmering through each December.
Crimson leaves floating in the sky.
How could I forget to remember?

Does the snow lie on Penshaw Monument?
Can you still see it glittering bright?
Let's all wish a Merry Christmas to Castletown tonight.
Angels sing their sweetest songs from the stars over Castletown tonight.

Does the cauld lad still roam the ruins by silent walls
By silent stones where gargoyles frown?
Are the bonny young golden boys
Still swallowed by the mine ~ going down ~ going down?

Do the children play in the liney
And fish the Wear from Baron's Quay?
Its grey water flow through the wind and the rain.
Please can I come back again?
Please can I come back again?

Let's all wish a Merry Christmas to Castletown tonight.
Angels sing their sweetest songs from the stars over Castletown tonight.

Elizabeth Stephens

Root Cause

I'll never leave the North East for no matter where I stray,
Whatever trips I take away my roots will here remain.
I'm anchored to Newcastle town where bridges cross the Tyne,
As it flows down to the piers on its journey into brine.
I always look for Penshaw perched high upon its hill,
Whenever trips return me home to where my heart lives still.
North Shields set on its river bank will always seem like home,
And South Shields with its market place where as a youth I roamed.
But most of all friends and folks will be always on my mind,
Their humour and their frankness is a very special kind.
Although the weather may be grim with North East winds so cold,
And my head may be in London still my feet will wander home.
To where I'm always welcome ~ a Geordie welcome's best,
My home is in their terraces where I know my feet will rest.
Though the journey's often longest which takes you home some day,
My roots are in that river bank and they'll bring me back to stay.

P Sanders

Nan's Promise
(In memory of Barbara Ann Miller)

Ha way my hinny
My bishy bairn
I'll keep you safe
I'll keep you warm
I'll dry your tears
I'll share your smiles
I'll sing to you
I'll stay awhile
'Til you grow up
To taste sweet pleasures from life's drinking cup.

Barbara Blyth

The Cheviots

I'm going to the Borders
And cannot wait to see
The Cheviots in their splendour
Mean everything to me.

The heather blooms so brightly
The ferns are way up high
And sheep that graze upon the hills
Are bleating to the sky.

I feel the past come creeping through
Whenever I am there
To never see them any more
Is more than I could bear.

I need to go and walk the earth
That thousands have walked before
To see the land stretched out below
And hear the Legions' roar.

How can I fail to marvel
At God's illustrious plan
To see the Cheviots once again
Just made for beast and man?

Valley of the River Alwin, The Cheviots, Northumberland

Joan M Lister

Penshaw Monument

The monument built on the top of Penshaw Hill, was designed on that of The Temple of Diana at Ephesus, but the proportions were doubled, and included a staircase in one of the columns. This has long been closed, because of a tragic accident, the only incident of its kind, since it was constructed.

The Earl of Durham's tenants, in recognition of his kindly acts and fairness to them, built the monument by raising subscription, and the designer, who lived and worked in Newcastle, was commissioned to draw up the plans.

John George was the Earl of Durham to whom this monument was erected, he was a Member of Parliament for Durham, held office of Lord Privy Seal, Ambassador Extraordinary, Minister of the Court of St Petersburg, and Governor General of Canada. He died July 28th 1840, aged 49 years.

Stone from local quarries was used, as was a lot of local labour. The job of laying the foundation stone was given to the Marquis of Zetland, who was Grand Master of the Free and Accepted Masons of England, on August 28th 1844.

The monument has an open roof, and local stories claim it was deliberately omitted for different reasons. The first, because, it is said that the Earl raised the rents on his tenants' cottages saying, 'If they can afford to build a monument, they can afford to pay me more rent,' to which the tenants replied, 'We winnet raise a roof 'cos the Earl has raised our rents.' Another tale told, is that the monument is not complete, because a statue of the Earl of Durham riding a horse, was supposed to go on top, but lack of funds prevent this, and the statue was given to Durham City instead. This is not true in fact, as the statue in the market place at Durham, is that of The Marquis of Londonderry. Also, the Earl of Durham had died four years previously, so why place someone else's statue on *his* monument?

Kenneth Crow

The New City

Take a boat from Roker two miles out to the sea
Look back at the coastline and see what is to be,
Gone are all the shipyards and the cranes have too
The wheel of Wearmouth Colliery completely
gone from view.

St Peter's church surrounded by the University
the houses and yachts in the marina by the sea.
Gone are the workmen Lowry portrayed with peaked,
cloth caps, the miners and fishermen, rat catchers
with their traps.

We're looking, yes, at Sunderland, England's newest
city, with all the new buildings is becoming rather pretty,
the bridges, the shopping centre attractively designed.
The convenience of the shoppers very much in mind.

Now we have students with jeans and trendy gear,
studying in Sunderland, confident and without fear,
students' accommodation multiplying and coming
into view. Very security conscious for young peoples'
safety too.

The local councils' planning the future to arrange, for
the people of this city welcome the gradual change,
looking forward, I am sure, are going to find Sunderland
University, a very special kind.

The golden sands of Roker and Seaburn bay, the
fairground, the Seaburn centre, entertainment every day.
Yes, Sunderland's progressing into a tourist attraction,
giving local people pride and satisfaction.

Christine Ridley Henderson

The Men Of South Shields

They built the ships and saw them glide
Out thro' the piers on the flowing tide.
Their sons were the sailors and many died ~
Serving King and country.

They mined for coal, father and son;
Deep in the earth 'til the shift was done.
Gasping for breath when their lungs were gone ~
Serving Queen and country.

Wars to be won? ~ These men were there.
Steadfast; courageous; doing their share.
Wives and bairns kneeling in prayer ~
Serving Queen and country.

Proud; independent; standing tall;
These are the Shieldsmen, brave men all ~
And there, 'Always Ready' for duty's call
To serve God and country.

V Finlay

Sunderland, Tyne And Wear, 2000

Where once, not so long ago, did stand
J L Thompson's, who built ships so grand,
Now, resides the University of Sunderland.

The old pier, and lighthouse, still sweep out to sea
But a new harbour, and marina, enhance it so prettily,
And the yearly air show is definitely, a sight to see.

No longer a town, but a city in its own right
With seafront illuminations that shine in the night
I guess Sunderland is doing all right.

Up to now, everything is going to plan
With all the car-making at Nissan
Anything, anywhere can achieve, Sunderland can.

Gordon Bannister

Untitled

My father at his shop in Hendon Road, Sunderland, which was a
well-known shopping area. The photograph as taken approx 1930.
My grandfather opened the business early 1900, which was taken
over by my father around 1925. When he died my brother carried on
until the area was redeveloped.

Mrs Halliday

Fear In A Dole Queue

Despondent people, eyes glazed with pain
Victims of a materialistic regime,
Empty humiliation ~ a fixed gaze
No perception in this deprived age,
No way forward in the ring of fear
Sorrow for my family, the ones I hold most dear.

The north's highest unemployment rate
And we're at the mercy of the State!

With entwining arms which once grew strong
The Tyne's powerful structure is all but gone!

Creative hands, mechanical skills
All grind to a halt
And like the grave ~
Pale, unfeeling, cold and still!

Margaret E Richards

The Oxo Hut

Geordie: Hey, Jonty, hev ye heard, they're gonna demolish the Oxo Hut that useter be in Sunderland Football Club's Roker Park ground . . .

Jonty: It sounds as if you've been readin' the Sunderland Echo again, bonny lad, are ye sure it's true?

Geordie: Wi, as a matter o' fact I've got the Echo here, Jonty, I'll read what it says:

> 'The Manager and Directors of Sunderland Football Club hev decided to sell off the Oxo Hut which stood proudly at Roker Park for over fifty years, allowin' supporters to hev a hot drink at half-time every time Sunderland were playin' a match at home . . . the hut will be broken down into 500 bits o' wood, an' each bit will be sold for £10 a bit, proceeds to the Manager's Fund for summer Holidays in Majorca for needy players only bein' paid twenty thousand pounds a week . . . priority will be given to Season Ticket Holders on production of their passport or driving licence or any other means of identification, as demand for these bits of wood is certain to be heavy . . . only one bit o' wood per person . . .'

Jonty: By gox, Geordie, that'll be a souvenir to treasure, ye cud make a frame for it an' hang it up on the wall o' yer bedroom, an' every time ye wake up of a mornin' ye cud luk at it an' think o' the times ye useter stand in a queue forra cup of Oxo, bonny lad . . . I wuddent mind a souvenir like that me'sel . . .

Geordie: Wi, if ye really want one, marra, I'll get our lad to get ye one, he's gorra season ticket an' 'e cud camp overnight outside the Roker Park souvenir shop to make sure 'e gets a bit o' wood when the shop opens . . . 'e cud chop the wood in half an' then ye cud each hev a bit, that means it'll only cost ye each a fiver . . .

Jonty: Gud idea, Geordie, ye think of everythin' . . . but I'm just thinkin' that if the wood's been knockin' around for fifty years, it's tied to be a bit rotten in parts, an' that means if I frame it, it'll just disintegrate, won't it? . . . I mean, ye cannot hev a pile o' wood dust framed an' hangin' on yer bedroom wall, can ye? . . .

Geordie: Wi, I suppose ye cud always get some wood preservative, Jonty, an' steep the wood in it overnight afore ye frame it, surely? . . . I mean, ye can get wood preservative these days what even kills woodworm, it cud keep the wood in gud condition forever, an' ye cud pass it on to yer grandchildren an' tell them it's part o' the Roker Park Oxo Hut what no longer exists, a bit o' local history what cud be worth a fortune in about 90 years' time, ye know, what they call a collector's item, like . . .

Jonty: I suppose ye're right, Geordie, 'cos I remember a few years ago, when the Berlin Wall came down, folks were fightin' one another to get bits o' stone from the wall so's they cud put it on display in thor houses an' say to thor grandchildren, 'that's a bit o' the Berlin Wall, hinney, it useter hev barbed wire on top an' soldiers wi' machine guns to stop folks crossin' from East to West Germany . . . by lad, yor grandchildren cud take bits o' the Roker Park Oxo Hut to school an' show thor friends . . . that wud be grand, mind . . .

Geordie: And they cud show their teachers as well, bonny lad, they cud say that thor grandad once useter drink Oxo outside the Hut at Roker Park when 'e watched the red-an-whites playin' the likes o' Manchester United an' Arsenal an' Aston Villa . . . ye know, when ye come to think about it, that's what education is all about . . .

Jonty: Well spoken, Geordie, an' ye know, ye cannit whack education, I remember when Tony Blair became Prime Minister in 1997, 'e said 'e was goin' to concentrate on three things . . .

Geordie: O aye, bonny land, an' what was the three things, like? . . .

Jonty: Education, education, an' education, marra . . .

Geordie: Wi, there's nee better education for the lads and lasses o' the North-East than the history o' Sunderland Football Club, an' there's neebody can deny that the Roker Park Oxo Hut has played a vital part in that history, now howway, Jonty, admit it . . .

Jonty: I certainly *do* admit it, Geordie, an' I've just been thinkin' I'm fairly sure me gran'father has a mug what 'e useter take with him into Roker Park to sup Oxo from, 'cos I believe there was never enough Oxo mugs to meet public demand, Sunderland was a very poor football club in the old days, they cuddent afford goalposts when they first started, they had to ask spectators for the loan o' thor jackets, an' the players had to pay a tanner (sixpence) a week to belong to the club, none o' this payin' players fifty thousand pund a week an' twenty million pund transfer fees like they do these days, bonny lad . . .

Geordie: Aye, they were *real* futballers in them days, Jonty, straight outa the pit an' kickin' a ball about for 90 minutes, an' they were lucky to gerra fiver . . .

Jonty: But mind, Geordie, they gorra free mug of Oxo at half-time, an' when they came to leave the Club, they gorra Golden Handshake, a fiver an' a souvenir Oxo mug, they didn't do badly when ye think about it, the likes o' you an' me got nowt for workin' in the pit . . .

Geordie: I suppose, bonny lad, like us, they were born fifty years too soon, they had to graft forra livin', the players these days aren't worth washers, yet they're millionaires afore they reach thor thirtieth birthday . . . ye cannit whack it, marra . . . sup up.

John Stephenson

Untitled

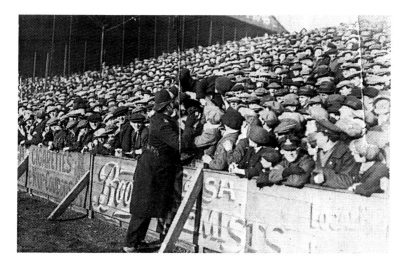

The photo depicts a person overcome by a crush of people being
rolled down over the heads of spectators who willingly assisted in
moving the victim down to the front of the stands, where they were
allowed to sit down with their backs to the fence until the end of the
game. This was a regular occurrence at Sunderland's matches.
Credit, Northern Echo.

John Wilkinson

A Day At The Seaside

There were five of us that beautiful summer's day, boys of ten years of age. Philip Wells, that was me, Tucker Armstrong, Norman Finnering, Charlie Marshal and Tommy Holmes. We had sat all of the day in the back lane, causing trouble most of the time. It had all started with a game of kick the can, the lane wasn't very wide, and to add to things it was Monday, and it was festooned with washing lines. The clothes were blowing in the summer breeze until we started kicking the can around. Tommy kicked it so hard that it went smack into my mother's clean clothes. She didn't find it very funny. I got a slap across the lugs, and all my so-called friends ran away, and left me to face the music.

I caught up with them later after my telling off. We were so bored, the school summer holidays had just started. We longed for adventure. Something different to do instead of hanging around the streets. We sat on the kerbside all in deep thought.

'I know, said Tucker, 'Let's go to the seaside.' The idea sounded great.

'But how will we get there, and who knows the way?' I asked.

'We just follow the tram lines,' said Norman. We sat in the street that day planning our great adventure.

'Don't tell anyone about our plans, or they will stop us from going,' I said, 'Let's meet outside Polly Peacock's, the grocers, at about 9 o'clock, and we should all bring something to eat, because it will be along day.'

Just before going our separate ways, we all pledged an oath not to tell a soul about our arrangement.

We all met the next morning, well everyone but Norman Finnering, he was always late, so we went around to seek him. He lived above the rag and bone man, the yard was always stinking with old rabbit skins. The skins were taken to him, and he would give you two pennies in return. A fresh rabbit on those days cost about sixpence with the skin on, or eight pence skinned by the butcher. That day the yard was high with the rotten smell, we covered our noses with our hands as we banged on the door for Norman. He was the smallest of us all, but not lacking in gob, kissed the Blarney Stone a few times we reckoned. His family were Irish, but had lived in

Shieldfield quite a long time. We eventually heard him coming down the stairs. His shoes made a terrible noise on the wooden floor.

'Sorry I'm late,' he said, 'but my mother caught me taking a wedge of bread. I told her I was hungry, but she said I was telling lies, and gave me a wallop, and some jobs to do before I could come out.'

'The devil will get your tongue,' we heard her shouting at the top of her voice after him; then the door banged. It echoed through the whole of the house, and we took off as fast as our legs would take us to find the tram line that led to the seaside.

It was now about 9.30am. We were a little later than expected, but no one cared, the day was bright, and beautiful, not a cloud to be seen, and we were so excited. The tram we knew went to North Shields so we knew that all we had to do was head for Byker, then Wallsend, on to North Shields, then Tynemouth, and then the sea and the sand. Some of the way we had to walk beside special tracks, and other times the lines were just on the roadside. The roads, were very narrow, and most of the traffic was horse-drawn. After a while we got a bit thirsty, and stopped to have a drink from one of the spa's that were set aside for watering the horses. I can still see Tommy washing the muck and sweat from his face. He was a bright ginger lad and burnt very easily with the sun, and he always looked so hot, and red-faced. We asked the conductor of one of the trams what time was it?

'Nearly half past twelve,' he said. 'And where, might I ask, are you lads going?' We all told him together, 'To the seaside.'

It must have been another hour after, that we started to feel a bit hungry. Poor Norman had nowt to eat, so we put all our food together, and shared it between the five of us. I had brought two thick slices of bread covered with jam, and wrapped in brown greaseproof paper, Tucker had brought some windfall apples (I didn't ask him whose garden they had come from). Tommy had brought some old chips from the night before's dinner. He had told his mother he was starving, and she had given him a double amount on his dinner plate, and when she had turned her back on him, he had put them into an old sweet bag. Charlie, who was the fattest of us all, had asked his mother for a picnic. 'We are going to the park,' he had told her. There was two hard-boiled eggs, a big slice of bread with butter on, and a big piece of rice cake. We sat down in a field nearby, spread our picnic on a khaki handkerchief, and ate the lot. We must have looked a funny sight that day following the tram line, and eating cold, soggy chips out of a sweet bag; horrible, but we were a happy lot.

It took us five hours, if I recollect, to walk to Tynemouth, but it was worth the long walk to catch sight of the sea for the first time.

I thought it was so blue, even nicer than I could have ever imagined, and it sparkled in the sunshine.

'It goes all the way to the sky,' said Charlie.

The sand was so warm, our black sand-shoes, and socks were off, and we ran like mad boys down to the shore line yelling, and shouting with excitement. We splashed around until we were exhausted, then lay on the sand recovering for some time; what an adventure we were having. Tommy went to look in some rock ponds, and found a little crab.

'I'm taking him home,' he said, 'he can go in the empty sweet bag.' In the crab went, then stuffed into his trouser pocket with all the other horrible things, hairy sweets, old bits of string, and even an old rabbit's foot.

'Supposed to be lucky,' he said, 'Norman gave it to me in exchange for one of my prize liggies.' (Marbles)

The North Sea was very cold on our little feet, even in the summer heat, so we buried them in the soft, warm sand, and it was great. How long we stayed down there I can't really say. We asked a gentleman walking his dog if he could tell us the time please, and were shocked to find it was almost tea time. No wonder our little stomachs were making noises like the sea. The time had come to wander back home, no one really wanted to go, the magic of the sea, and the sand, still had control of us.

Charlie was the first to announce his stomach was aching through lack of food, and we had better start back home. His mother would be out looking for him knowing how much he enjoyed eating. The food he had taken was only a snack, not enough for all day, and he'd had to share it among the others. It was now well after four in the afternoon.

We dried our feet on our socks, no one had brought a towel, then on went the black sand-shoes, our feet felt very rough for walking, and five hours later they were very sore. The socks, being still wet, decorated our shoulders.

We looked like a little army marching back along the tram line, tired, and very hungry. Five hours later we arrived back at Lowry Street. It was just starting to get dark, as we turned the corner, we plucked up enough strength and courage to sing 'Here we are, Here we are, Here we are again.' The sight that greeted us was by far the most frightening moment I can remember. The street was out in force. Mothers, fathers, sister, brothers, aunties, grandmothers, you name it, they were out there looking for the lost children (us).

Our families went mad with us, but we didn't really care if we were mordered (murdered).

'We will take you to the polus (policeman) in the morning, he knows what to do with bad lads,' shouted mother. The polus would take his gloves out of his belt and hit you hard across the head and ears, it would sting for a while, and you would be the talking point in Shieldfield for a week or two, but who cared? All we wanted was something to eat, a nice cup of hot tea, and sleep.

That summer's day is still so fresh in my memory, but that's not quite the end of the story. Next day Tommy Holmes's mother was about to wash his sandy trousers, and when she emptied his pockets, she found a piece of string, a smelly rabbit's foot, and an empty, sticky, greasy, damp sweet packet, but on the floor of the scullery, right next to her foot, was the biggest spider she had ever seen. Its claws were huge, and it had the biggest goggly eyes that watched her every move.

What a scream she gave out. Everyone through she had been on the gin again, and didn't believe a word of it.

When Tommy told us the story, we laughed for ages, we knew it was only a crab, a little one at that!

Maureen Spencer

Hendon Flats

The Phoenix rose from the ashes,
No more clashes of falling bombs,
Haphazard, new-fangled building,
Accompanied heartening songs.

A bit repaired here, and some rebuilt there,
Demolished, dug out and in-filled,
Planners ran riot, building amok,
Reviving a heart almost stilled.

'We must have the new, not the good or the bad.
We must build it wide, build it tall.'
Those towers and courts, once pristine, once true,
Were destined to topple and fall.

To clear it all up, and build life anew,
Replace hovels and social decline,
Those planners did try in their limited way,
Their Nemesis really was time.

Wendy Tetley

An Empty Shell

An empty shell, washed up
By the banks of the Tyne.
Mountains of rubble sand
Strewn with bits and bobs.
Decrepit old yards,
Half buildings and metal scraps.
Once the pride of those
Touched by time
Is use to no one,
Is wasted land.
A little lad's dream factory.
An island for him to play.
Pirates searching hidden pebbles
Kicked behind a metal bin.
His ruins.
Grandad welded ships together
Over there,
By the gap in the railings.

Rachael Widdrington

Memories

South Shields is a pleasant town
Though changed in many ways,
Older folk reflect on times
Before these changes were made.

Ocean Road then had many shops
An inviting place to be,
Children would gaze wistfully
At all that they could see.

Buckets, spades and fishing nets
High up out of reach,
Needed by the children
To play with on the beach.

Passing these Aladdin's caves
Onward to the fair,
Mounting excitement
As music filled the air.

Juke Boxes blaring
All the latest tunes
The sea in the distance
Beyond sand dunes.

People thronging eagerly
For rides that scared and thrilled,
Small hands clutching buckets
That with sand would soon be filled.

Ships passing between the Piers
The Gateway to the Tyne,
A pleasant sight to see
When the weather was fine.

Watching from the Groyne
One could almost leap aboard,
Plenty to see and do
So that no-one got bored.

A walk back through the park
Watching boys with boats on the lake,
Then a trip back home on a Trolley Bus
Because it was getting late.

Seeing queues outside the cinemas
Which were dotted around the town,
Pubs filled with thirsty people
Which to youngsters were out of bounds.

A few things have gone
Since those happy days,
No treasure-filled shops
In which children would gaze.

Just restaurants now for adults
And a quiet river.
Progress changes many things
And not always for the better.

M F Wakefield

The Lighthouse On St Mary's Island, Whitley Bay, And The Sea

You were the warning light for seafarers in mortal plight of me.

I am the sea, I reign supreme,
lapping, surging, welling, heaving,
lashing, whipping, to and fro, unending.
Often hated, welcomed, used,
sometimes friend, sometimes foe,
from icy wastes to humid shores, I am there.
Eating away at crumbling cliffs,
or flooding arid plains,
my vapour rising, and as rain falling
I am everywhere.
Children splashing in the shallows,
ships wrestle raging waves,
sea life wallows in deep waters
where a human life drowns.
I hide the murky sea bed, and spew up tracts of land,
I am indispensable to existence,
I am the life force.

Now no more your light shines bright,
but standing proud, and tall and white,
reminder of the endless fight,
with me.

   Judith Ruddy

Three Giants Of Industry

Three giants of industry still in demand
Have ceased to be in Sunderland
Shipbuilding, mining, brewing of beer
Will no more be seen upon the Wear.

Who would believe in this day and age
Greed and stupidity was still all the rage?
With mindless fatcats who don't give a damn
And have taken the lifeblood from Sunderland.

So will the last man leaving the shipyard
Please close the door?
For not one more ship will be launched anymore
And will the last man leaving the pithead
Please close the door?
For not one piece of coal will be mined anymore
To the last man leaving the brewery
Please close the door
For not one pint of beer will be brewed anymore

Three giants of industry still in demand
Have been laid to rest in Sunderland.

J Kelly

Sunderland Revisited

Azalea terrace, south and north, thoughts of youth, good and bad.
I remember well what they were worth, happiest days I have ever
                                                                had.
Late for school, the clock's struck nine, teacher smiles; he's feeling
                                                                grand.
What the hell, I still feel fine, even after three of his best, on each
                                                                hand.

Finished school now, got a job, yet still I'm wondering what to think,
Proved them wrong, I'm not a yob; I'm dancing with the best girl in
                                                                the Rink.
My Saturday nights are fully booked, doing the barn-dance in the
                                                                hall.
Hepworth's suit on, how smart I looked, dancing better than Bobby
                                                                Knoxall.

Football mad now, no time for girls, we have lost again, still, never
                                                                mind.
Roker Park trials to show my curls. 'You're still too small, lad,' back to
                                                                the grind.
Joined up now for foreign parts, Tommy Steele was singing the blues,
I left the girls with broken hearts; Elvis is going on about blue shoes.

Home again, all seems changed, Mill steps have gone, no short cut
                                                                now.
No town hall clock to race against, the Ivy house, not the same
                                                                somehow.
No Johnson Street, where true love shone, my old friends have all
                                                                departed,
The town I loved and left is gone, yet I'm back again, where it all
                                                                started.

The Rosslyn babes are no longer tapping, the town's demise is such a
pity,
Empire crowd has stopped clapping, and some fools have made our
town a city.
City status run by a village mind, like a headless chicken running
around
The same old problems, it's so unkind, smiling faces cannot now be
found.

Things may not be as bad as they appear, so shed no tears for days
gone by.
Remember the best of yesteryear; we know too well how time can fly.
Just grab your memories by the hand and don't ever let them fade
away.
Be happy for days in old Sunderland remember, because tomorrow's
just another day.

George Hutchinson

HUMBERSIDE

In Scawby Woods

A grey gull's nest lies in the wood
Where Devil's Bit and Filbeards hide,
The twig has lost the warming breast
That moved the Helibore beside
Her circled leaves and badger fur,
And the dead bark that winters bring
Shelter to an ageing thin white web
That fluffs her empty wing.

A grey gull's shadow haunts the ground
Where ploughs turn topsoil from the sun
And further to the glow of steel
They circle black on white, but one
Half seeing, saw in the distant wood
Well sheltered and half full of leaves
Her nest caught in the damp of evening
That the mist finger weaves.

A grey gull's nest, unwanted still,
Over the bog and bracken flame,
Where saffron threads of winter fill
Each loneliness, beneath the same
Broad sky of bush and tree
That bends each turret bough in vain
To urge, as Celandine the sun,
A grey gull back again.

W E Hobson

Steel Town

In the inky darkness
The molten glow is as the setting sun,
Unnatural, eerie, out of place.
That picture illuminates
The corridors of distant memory.
But I see further along
The undercurrent of that liquid light
Shines in proud splendour.
Across five continents,
An unlikely dispersion
From this garden centre of Lincolnshire.
Its homely mix of park, mart and mall
And laid back, easy-going populace.
Belying the rich, mineral strata
That formed the lifeblood here.
The butt of many a jest and pun
Returns with interest the fun.
Its steely flow of fulfilled ambition
Finds answered dreams.

Colin Ella

Beverley Westwood
(Written in East Riding Dialect)

So they're talkin' o' fencing' off Westwood,
Did thoo ivver 'ear such a fond plan,
To stop cattle roamin' across roads
An' 'inderin' oor modern man.

Cattle ev rooamed about pasture,
Fer very nigh eight 'undred years
But foaks are impatient and hurried
An' it all offen ends up i' tears.

Cars flee on at fifty or sixty,
When they out ti be deein much less,
An' when they collide wi a bullock,
They end up in 'ell of a mess.

They've tried luminous collars on cattle,
An' talked aboot luminous socks,
They've discussed all soorts o' speed 'umps,
Mebbe answer is cow muck road blocks.

Why can't foaks just gan a bit steady,
An' drahve wiv a little bit more care,
An' beath man an beast'll live together.
Then we'll 'ave peace on Westwood yance mair.

Westwood's been a grand spot fer picnics,
There's foaks out just walking their old dogs,
I' wartime the' went there for firewood
An' kem oam wi' prams full o' good logs.

It'll 'inder foaks wi' their picnics,
Or gannin ti fly their kids' kites,
An' bairns off gannin sledgin' doon 'illsides,
An' all foaks on their posh mountain bikes.

Mebbe cattle'l nut understand it,
They'd much rather ev 'ad some speed 'umps,
If yon posts are big an' strang eneeaf,
They'll use 'em fer scratchin' their rumps.

Fences we can deea wivout 'em,
Let's just leave yon grand spot as it is,
It's a wonderful oppen green pasture,
I offen gans doon there for a ziz.

Mark Saxby

Kingston-Upon-Hull

Oh, Kingston fair upon the Hull
Just what creates your magic pull?
For, as a bird flies home to nest
If you're from Hull, that's where you'll rest.

As you approach our city fair
And see the flowers planted there,
Along the verges wide, and green,
Our pride in Hull can thus be seen.

Is it perhaps our city hall?
A place so grand, but that's not all
Acoustics there are of the best,
Where music soothes the savage breast.

Its organ too, of worldwide fame,
Played by those of wide acclaim.
Composers round the walls outside
Appear to listen with much pride.

Or, could it be our fine guildhall?
Its beauty which will never pall.
A building ~ proud, if you need proof.
See the adornments on the roof.

The corridors, both long and wide,
Those grand stairways, up inside.
The constant meetings, always full,
Control the pounding heart of Hull.

Or is it our historic past?
That makes our feet turn home at last
To view once more, to stop, and stare
At churches, or King Billy, or Victoria Square.

Go where you will, it matters not
If fame, or fortune, you have got,
When things begin to get you down
Come back to Hull ~ your own home town

R L Shipp

The Village Smithy

A cheery smile and open face
We see the smithy in his village place
In the forge, built from Yorkshire stone
There with horse, never alone.

This man so special in demand
Our horses care of feet command
For rich and poor it means the same
To hunt or jump and show we claim.

Whilst sinewed hands work with humble skill
He moulds their hooves ~ such a thrill
Great talent to all he does extend
No task too trivial, a duty to the end

Burning embers reflect in sparks, so few
He trims then files whilst bellows spew
Nudging and pushing seems a horse's sin
Gently he hammers the final nail in

The forge a sacred aim for horse
For many a common cause
To make our horses feet feel sublime
An inspiring craft used in present time

Grateful thanks we now say
Hand waving sends us on our way
'The Village Smithy'
Will remain the talk for many a day.

Victoria Margaret Revell

October At The 'Mere'

October moon is shining ~
Silhouetted on the Mere ~
The season now is passing by
And winter's drawing near.

Boats wallow at the water's edge ~
Terns glide by tranquilly ~
The Whooper Swan in sombre mood ~
Slumbers so nonchalantly.

Ripples on the surface dance,
When ~ October moon peeps out ~
Glittering the silver crests
As they skip all about.

The gentle waters lap the shore.
All around the season sleeps,
The year is now fast waning,
Nearer the winter creeps.

Malcolm Bucknall

Skidby Mill

You lie peacefully at anchor, a stately
galleon amidst the green ocean of fields.
Your white billowing sails turn steadily
and majestically against the peacock sky;
Whilst your heavy stones grind out the
bread of life.
Craftsmen demonstrate their skills and sell
their wares beneath your sheltering gaze;
And excited children clamber up your wooden
ladders to seek out your secrets.
You have seen so many changes through the
years yet your impassive face has merged for
all time; the hearts and souls of those who
spent their lifetimes in your service.
Your existence combines the past and present;
Today and the future.
Your whirling sails are the tick of centuries
over in a moment.

Chris Senior

NORTH YORKSHIRE

The Scarbora' Map

Gall and Inglis

Wonderful name, isn't it? . . . that was the company who produced the map, 25 Paternoster Square, London. The map was of Scarborough . . . or . . . Scarbora' as his owner would have said, for there it is for all to see, his name and address after all this time. This fantastic old map was owned by Wilfred Mainprize, also written in his own hand, his old address, where the old trams passed his front door, he lived in town, Prospect Road, which I'm sure will be of great interest to many people. This family is a well-renown and respected, still in town . . . but the story is of The Scarbora' Map. It is of great interest, will be, to collectors, not for its value, it's tattered and torn . . . well, let's say . . . not mint condition. The cover is wonderful, was this mistake ever pointed out to the printers, all those years ago when everything was hand set, the typographer, the boy . . . or . . .man, did he realise he didn't have a C and put in O instead, reading now, Tourist and Cyolists instead of Cyclists on the front cover? I treasure it for that alone, however it is a minefield of information, for anyone seeking information of Old Scarbora'.

In my possession, also presumably belonging to Wilfred, as I purchased them both at the same time in an old book store, from the same bundle, but no name on this one. Bacon's large-scale plan of *Scarborough*, from another London printers . . . this map has some great information, of old Scarbora', of special interest, showing the central schools, Victoria Street, and, on the opposite side of the road, the workhouse and the prison, mapped, where the registrar's office was on Dean Road.

The two toll-houses, are mapped on Marine Drive, one of which is still standing. An excellent example of architecture of the period, a wonderful round building, complete, I am told with the existing windows for paying the tolls to enter or exit, after viewing the seafront.

This brings us up to date, with the current issue, raging in Scarborough, and of particular interest to the current officers in the town planning, their brief . . . (perhaps) . . . to reinstate the other one. Yes! A wonderful way to take the coffers from all and sundry, residents and visitors alike, who may wish to view our wonderful coastline, not forgetting the extra charge for . . . actually stopping . . . to view the horizon. This will delight, also, the newly recruited army of parking officers, just in case anyone escaped lightly first time, and when this project is complete there will be much rubbing of hands, back slapping and sighs of delight in the council quarters.

I was especially interested in the rocks of North Bay, and would be interested to hear if anyone knows the story of Betty Muffett Rocks, which seems to lay in the region opposite to the position marked for the old barracks on the North Bay.

Tracey Spencer

The Market

Step down,
From the Pennine bus
Onto rain glazed setts
And I am in Skipton town.
To root around
The tangled order
Of rails and racks.
'You Know Whose'
Slight seconds.
Danielle Steel, Catherine Cookson
In cut price stacks.
Wishing on the spine
The author's name
Was mine.
'Half a pound of Wensleydale
with blueberries please.'
I receive, two hundred grams.
Would Stevie prefer South Park
Or Simpsons pyjama set?
He won't get either
When I read the irreverent
Yet wittily subversive slogan.
Passing by the CD stall
And Bob Will's voice
Fills two nostalgic minutes.
A wok or frying pan?
To buy from the kitchen man.

A marrow chilling wind
Decides that I,
Cross the road,
For a coffee and bacon butty
In the fleamarket cafe.
As Sir Mathew Wilson sternly stares
And almost declares:
'Tha can't move in Skipton today
Because market's on.'

Wendy Milner

Untitled

Burton Agnes Church

June E Harrison

Swaledale

I love to walk up Swaledale
Over the hills where peace does prevail,
To climb up a hill, admire the view
And marvel at what the Lord can do.

Just to pause, be still and rest
In the presence of One who gives only the best,
With sheep gently grazing and lambs at play,
Walking the dales is my kind of day.

Elizabeth Tomlinson

The Hispaniola

I must have been about six years old, dressed in a blue cotton pinafore-dress with a red cagoule to keep off the summer showers and buckled sandals with closed-in toes. I stood by the edge of the Mere, at Seamer, looking skyward at a very tall, jolly pirate, who was smiling down from his great height. He was chuckling, as I supposed at the time, in the way that pirates would, his black eye patch slipping as he laughed, revealing, rather disappointingly, a perfectly healthy eyeball. I ran up the short gangplank onto the pirate ship, without caution, as six-year-olds do, with my mother behind me looking slightly alarmed at my abandon.

The Hispaniola was ready to set sail. The voyage was filled with sounds of creaking wood and children's busy feet as we ran in hyperactive, dizzy circles, high on tartrazine orange lollipops that the pirate with the healthy eyeballs had handed to us once aboard. Mothers looked on protectively to ensure their children didn't dive overboard into the murky shallow waters below. The same waters where, a fortnight before, I had watched as my father had spectacularly sunk his lovingly crafted miniature boat operated by remote control. An hour later, he had managed to fish it out, retrieving his once beautiful boat, now clogged with slimy last year's leaves and a few rusting bottle tops.

The pirate flag was hoisted high, fluttering in the breeze as a warning to the island ahead of the impending invasion of loud, small people. Sunlight illuminated brightly coloured rain jackets scampering across the secret island where our pirate and his mate had deposited us. Sugar jewels nestled like treasure amongst leaves and logs. It felt like a tropical paradise, all exotic, lush and secret. Piles of huge golden doubloons lay in wait for our small hands to snatch and bundle into pockets as booty to take back to shore.

At least, that's how I like to remember it. Twelve years later, I spotted the boat languishing forlornly by the outdoor swimming pool at the North Bay, bereft of the magic I remembered. It looked tiny, a rotting relic with peeling varnish, that meant nothing to the tourists who passed it without a second glance on the way to the ice-cream kiosk for a '99'. Then it just disappeared.

This summer, as I watched the speedboats skimming across the South Bay in the sunshine, a slower vessel, catching the swell of the North Sea, caught my eye. Like a long lost friend, so familiar yet in unfamiliar surroundings, the salt water was lapping the life back into the old Hispaniola timbers, thankfully rescued and restored for the sea by local fishermen. Several times a day, in and out of the harbour, it curls under the gaze of the lighthouse, taking new crews of adventurers searching for their Treasure Islands.

Virginia Welford

Changes In Rural Life

I live in the small village of Burniston which lies five miles north of Scarborough and straddles the road to Whitby. It is a delightful place to live being situated in beautiful countryside close to the North Sea cliffs, which are eroding due to Global Warming, the North Yorkshire Heather Moors and extensive forests.

Cars, which mean people can commute large distances, have ruined village life. People have moved into the village, wooed by its rural charms and then these same people try to change the very things that brought them here in the first place. The village had more than doubled in size due to new homes being built. Because of cars and Privatisation, the Local Bus Service has been drastically reduced. We now have no serviced after 19.15 from Monday to Saturday and none at all on a Sunday so unless someone in the family has a car, we are no longer able to participate in activities in Scarborough or go to Nigh Classes there. Because of Supermarkets, we now only have one Village Shop and Post Office with a very limited range of goods. We have lost a Butcher's Shop, a Cobbler's Shop and a very good General Store. The Railway Line to Whitby had just closed when we came to live here but at least the Council purchased it for walkers and cyclists and it is a haven for wild life. We often see deer on the line. Ease of travel and cheap flights have seen the end of the Bed and Breakfast Trade which was once a thriving business.

There is now only one working farm in the village where there used to be five and now Dairy Herds no longer block the village streets when they are being brought to the farms for milking. The Farm Labourer's Cottages are now let as Holiday Homes and Farm Buildings have been turned into desirable houses. More arable crops such as rape and potatoes are grown on land that was once used mostly for grazing. The allotments have gone as people would rather spend their spare time making their gardens attractive with bedding plants and hanging baskets than grow their own fruit and vegetables which are now cheap to buy. Many people still pick sloes to make gin and brambles for jam and pies and blossoms, flowers and fruit for wine. We still have a Country Show every August Bank Holiday Monday and we have had a WI Show in September for the last nine years.

Wild flowers are now protected by law, so primroses and bluebells are prolific and cowslips have returned to our hedgerows as the farmers no longer cut them back and the use of some sprays are banned. There are many wild animals in the vicinity including badgers, foxes, roe deer, squirrels, newts, hedgehogs and rabbits. The bird population, especially thrushes and blackbirds, are decreasing and a cuckoo is seldom heard these days. Voles have almost disappeared from the streams but otters have been reintroduced and recently a kingfisher flew up the stream which runs around the bottom of our garden. Over the last few years there have been very few fish in the beck perhaps because of this we do not see the heron very often.

A strong sense of Community still exists and there is much to do in the village for people of all ages. The Village Hall has a Children's Playing Field, Tennis Courts and Bowling Green. The Hall is used for Country and Western Dances, a Youth Club, Evergreen Club, Bingo, Badminton, Whist Drives, Table Top Sales, Jumble Sales and WI Meetings. The School is no longer only for the children of this village. It serves the surrounding area. We still have two local inns which serve food as people eat out more these days. Both Inns have Darts and Domino Teams. There is a Village Cricket Team but we no longer have a Football Team. The Chapel and Church, in the next village, work together. Between them they have two Sunday Schools, a Boys Brigade, a J-Team, a Mother's Union and Fellowship Group. There is also a Mothers and Toddlers Group and regular Chapel Coffee Mornings and Monthly Chapel Lunches, where I used my newly acquired Waitress Skills. We have just had our first Lady Vicar. The Baptist Church is now a house. The Doctor's Surgery and The Blacksmith's Shop are found in the next village as our Blacksmith's Shop closed some time ago. Fewer horses are shoed these days. The Blacksmiths mostly make wrought iron articles and do various repairs.

A small industrial estate has been developed on the outskirts of the village and some years ago Gas Pipes were brought to the village, which have made coal fires the exception rather than the rule these days.

Even in the thirty years that I have lived here, the village life has changed dramatically. I often wonder what life will be like here at the end of the next thirty years?

Ruth Malton

The Lost Fountain

This beautiful, elegant Victorian fountain once stood in the market place in Richmond, North Yorkshire.

At some time in the late 40s it was taken to pieces and removed to make way for cars and buses.

It was almost forgotten until 1995 when someone had the idea of rebuilding it. A search was made, and gradually, all the lost pieces were found in lock-ups and storage rooms.

After viewing suitable locations, it was decided to place it outside the town museum where it now resides in all its Victorian splendour for the world to see and admire.

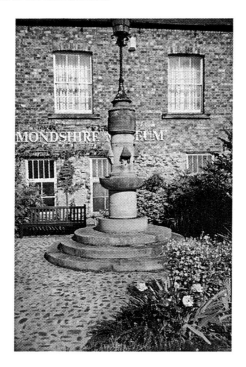

Edith Elliott-Sunter

Scarborough

What is it that I love about Scarborough? Everything ~ from the fun rides and donkeys, to the fascinating museums.

This historic town provides first class entertainment of theatre, variety shows, and musical venues, throughout the year. All hobbies and interests are catered for, the inhabitants friendly, kind, and welcoming to strangers.

Explore the surrounding countryside to discover forests, dales, vast moorland; plus abbeys, county towns, and attractive villages. An extensive network of public transport is available to take the strain.

One cannot help but admire the elegant, gracious architecture, glorious gardens, and stimulating, and invigorating walks. My favourite of these begins on the Esplanade; meandering through the Rose Garden to the enchanting Italian Garden; down the Chine to the disused swimming pool, where I learned to dive! If you are fortunate, you may stand silently, in wonder of a pair of herons on the rocks there.

Onward, passing the Spa, you may feel the rustle of an Edwardian gown on the breeze. Gazing at jostling boats in the harbour, beneath an ancient castle of an old walled town, you may hear the creak of Viking oars, or glimpse a shadowy ghost of a bygone sailing ship in the mist. Striding out round the Marine Drive to the accompaniment of screeching seagulls, you may experience the thrill of dodging waves of over forty feet high, crashing over the road to the foot of the headland. A foolhardy sport; take care.

After a welcome cuppa and a scone at the Corner Café, a stroll past colourful beach huts, left through Northstead Manor Gardens, will bring you to Peasholm Park. These delightful serene gardens of Oriental design, surround a lake of graceful swan paddle-boats, and brass-bandstand, and leads to the oasis of Peasholm Glen.

It is difficult to imagine oneself in a seaside resort when sauntering beneath these huge shady trees, alongside a sparkling stream of waterfalls, where the only sounds to be heard are those of birdsong, and gurgling water sliding over smooth stones. It is possible, if lucky, to spot a kingfisher here, and you are certain to be mugged by squirrels; better to have some peanuts ready.

The magic of Scarborough for me, is paddling, and crabbing on my way into town shopping. Cricket on the beach when my grandchildren visit. Waking every day with that 'holiday' feeling.

Taking an ice-cream on to the balcony at the Spa Theatre during the interval, listening to the swish of surf sucking pebbles dry, entranced by a dancing, crystal moonbeam path across dark waters to silvery sands.

I make no apologies for waxing lyrical in praise of my lovely Lady of Arcadia.

Ruth Judge

The Library

Life in 1940 Selby was a far cry from the half-deserted streets of today. I was forever dodging the legs and feet of a heaving mass of humanity and every shop except Woolworths and Piper's Penny Bazaar seemed to have a permanent queue. Sure there was a war on and it was a time of rationing but without fridges and freezers people tended to buy basic foodstuff from day to day, so the average sorties into town for Mother and I would be two or three times a week. A weekly must included with the shopping, was a visit to the Library to change Dad's library books.

The Library, at that time, was in James Street on the site of what now is the back entrance to the In Shops. It was a gaunt red brick Victorian edifice run, or rather ruled, by Miss Proctor who must have formed the original mould from whom all other librarians had been cast. With a voice that could cut glass at ten paces and a look designed to shrivel small boys in their boots she was truly fearsome, no less to grown-ups.

Physically her assistant, Miss Dobson, was everything Miss Proctor wasn't, tall, slim, with long blonde hair. She had everything going for her but true to the tradition of librarians all her attributes were carefully played down. Her long hair was drawn back in a Victorian bun, as if to emulate her superior. A permanent frown clouded her face that only needed horn-rimmed glasses to complete the perfect typecasting.

Clutching my Mother's hand we entered the hallowed precincts and joined the short queue to get our returned books checked back in. For me, books were an unknown quantity. Those we brought back had nothing in them to play with or even pictures to look at, just a mass of black marks on every page which for some reason Dad would sit staring at for hours at a time.

We were honoured by Miss Proctor's attendance upon us who greeted my Mother with a watery smile. I stared up at her with wide-eyed innocence and she glared back with barely concealed malevolence. She regarded children as mobile units of noise, trouble and mayhem and I was obviously no exception. The perfect child, to her way of thinking, would be garnished with salt and pepper and have an apple stuck in its mouth.

After passing her preliminary inspection we made our way to the novels section where Mother was soon engrossed. As there was nothing else I could do, I watched the two librarians and the customers with vague disinterest. Miss Proctor booked them in and Miss Dobson booked them out. Every so often Miss Dobson would cross over to Miss Proctor, who was standing a good five feet away, and whisper something conspiratorially in her ear. Silence was the golden rule, not even to be broken by Miss Proctor or her co-regent. For one wild moment I had an overpowering desire to let out an ear-splitting yell but the ramifications of such a barbarous act, even to one of my tender years, was too horrible to contemplate, besides my legs were beginning to ache.

On turning round to ease my throbbing limbs I found the solution staring me in the face. A small section of the bottom shelf was empty, just wide enough to fit in one small boy's bottom. Stretching myself to the full, I eased my backside into the vacant space and shuffled into place. It made a remarkably comfortable seat and I was just settling back to view the world anew when my end of the shelf collapsed and I was thrown against the side as it hit the floor. Books rained onto me but worse was to come as I had dislodged the end of the shelf above which pivoted down and away from me but cascaded perfectly every last book onto the pile already there.

Being more than a little dazed and up to my neck in books I was unable to appreciate the wrath of Miss Proctor that I had now unleashed. It would be many years before Mother filled me in on the gory details which time has drawn a hazy veil over, but it was Miss Proctor's parting shot that I would never forget.

As we left the building with heads hung in shame, her immortal last words rang in my ears, ' . . . And don't bring him in here again.'

Terry Brown

View Of The Flooded River Ouse In Central York

John F Fagan

Rock Solid

This is the house
A wise man built,
Well founded
On the rock-like
Promises
Of God.

No enemy assault,
Of any kind
Can penetrate
Its strong defence.

The Lord shall be
Its sure security,
And He will keep
In perfect peace
Each one
Who lives
Within its walls
Until that final move
To Heaven.

From a house at Hawes, in Wensleydale, North Yorkshire

Eileen Williams

My Village

My village lies in a shallow basin on the bleak, windswept moorland of North Yorkshire with heather-clad hills rising to 1000ft all around. As far as the human content is concerned there is nothing remarkable. We have our share of saints and sinners, busybodies and recluses; of gossip and scandal, neighbourliness and enmities and as many religious, political and moral persuasions as any other collection of Homo Sapiens. Only the setting is different ~ and therein lies the rub . . .

First it was Emmerdale, then Summer Wine and Herriot country ~ now it's the turn of my village, Goathland, in its guise as Aidensfield, to hit the tourist jackpot due to the success of the television series 'Heartbeat'. And not to everyone's delight either. While publicans, tea room and guesthouse proprietors, tour operators and shopkeepers are reaping the benefits of the upsurge in visitor trade, others are bewailing the increase in traffic, the spoiling of the verges and the village greens by an excess of parked vehicles and the loss of privacy as the visitors peer into gardens and windows trying to identify the police house, doctor's surgery, village pub, Greengrass's farm, etcetera.

It is a fact that the majority of these transitory visitors see the village and its environment only through the TV eye. They may exclaim at the beauty of the heather as they drive across the moors in August but they do not venture afield to explore the secluded river valleys. They may bask in warm sunshine as they picnic on the common but when the sea fret rolls in they do not stay to wonder at the chill eerieness of it. They may glimpse with a shudder the black bleakness of the moors in winter but they do not discover the hidden byways and the secrets of the woods. They cannot feel the thrill of hearing the first curlew in spring ~ such a plaintive cry but what a leap of the heart and soaring of the spirit at the sound of the 'Coorlyi' called on a rising note of expectation, wild and free and hopeful. Neither can they feel the sadness of bidding farewell to the plover and wagtail in autumn or the pleasure of welcoming the visiting bramblings and snow buntings. They will not see the beauty of the blackthorn blossom borne on black, leafless branches. Nor will they glimpse the elusive fox and roe deer in the woods or the adder and lizard on the moor.

The attitude of the 'Heartbeat' groupies was aptly exemplified by one gent in particular who, after his first ~ and probably last ~ visit was heard to remark, 'Who'd want to live up here? It's just miles and miles of b***** all.'

Well, maybe it is if you can't see past what you're looking at and won't try to identify the minutiae that make up the whole!

Jean Collins

Scarborough Lighthouse

To me there is no finer sight
Than Scarborough lighthouse in bright sunlight
Standing there, so proud and serene
Looking down on the busy scene
Cobbles and keelboats, sailing out to sea
And seagulls calling intermittently
This well-loved sight before my eyes
Only makes me realise
How much I love this town of my birth
This special place ~ this heaven on Earth
So much natural beauty here
As I gaze at the cliffs from my seat on the pier
My thoughts return to winter days
When storm-lashed piers are swept by waves
What a heart-warming sight the lighthouse must be
To the fishermen tossed on the stormy sea
The piers stretch out like welcoming arms
To enfold the ships where the sea is calm
The peace of the harbour casts its spell
And the lighthouse looks down saying,
'All is well.'

M Corrie

Unspoken Thoughts
(The disused Airfield at Riccall, near Selby)

Beyond the disused airfield, sheep grazed
Where Nissen huts long, low and grey,
Crouched half-hidden by the silver birch
And bracken, desolate in the sun's first ray.
Overgrown by tangled vine and bramble
Winding paths led nowhere in the lonely place.
And memories and the scent of death still lingered
As unseen ghost breath touched my face.
And for the men whose dreamless future
Ended in some distant blood-soaked mound,
Time wept and sighed with deep regret
But uneasy feelings came with little sound.
I wandered where the moss and tufted grass
Had reclaimed the weathered concrete hue,
And my sombre thoughts remained unspoken
For in my grateful heart I knew
I breathed the purest air of freedom
Beneath dear England's pale blue sky.
And for the nameless men, the bravest men,
I prayed, in the stillness of a last goodbye.

Rosamund Hudson

My World

Looking out of my window
I see the mist on the lake
Then I see the geese waiting at the gate.
I must put the kettle on and find my cups
As by now there will also be the ducks.
The white one is special, I must whistle him
Then find the nuts for the birds
I must feed them.
The moles let us know they are here
By leaving a mound in the lawn I fear.
The moorhen is timid and runs away in fright,
Soon the sun will go down and it will be night.
The lights come on, we look out of the house
Near the bird stand below is a mouse.
She is looking for food to feed her brood
They are in their nest, she just does her best.
The dogs are barking they have been disturbed
We look out to check before we go to bed.
The fox will come to visit, maybe also kill
I am afraid it is nature, I know he will.
The animals bring pleasure, we enjoy at our leisure.
These are things you cannot buy
Just to enjoy, you write with a sigh.

J E Moore

The Yorkshire Coast

Yorkshire, Yorkshire, why visit? I hear you say
Scarborough is well worth a journey to any day
The North Sea is always a very welcoming sight
Calm at times but then rough, frothy and white
There's the Castle, Spa and a lot of history to see
Then it's to a nice cafe for a pot of Yorkshire tea
Locally caught fish is tasty and hard to beat
The choice is amazing and there's plenty to eat
The North and South Bays are ideal for a walk
It's a nice atmosphere for a proposition or light-hearted talk
The County Cricket Ground is a lovely place to be at
It's a good arena to watch the best Yorkshire players bat
Italian ice-cream makers have been around forever
Their skills and choice of flavours are incredibly clever
The sea is a safe and secure area to take a dip
After a swim, it's a good choice to take a speedboat trip
It's a good idea to travel up to Robin Hood's Bay
The picturesque scene will take your breath away
All in all you'll have the time of your life
It's the ideal region to introduce to the kids and the wife

Paul Hudson

God's Yorkshire B & B

'Tis said when came the seventh day, that God lay down to rest,
but what I found they didn't say, is where He made His nest,

> now the rumour was, when His work was done,
> He did with nature talk,
> and then lay down 'neath the fading sun,
> in the beautiful vale of York,

where finding a place to lay His head, to nature He was heard to say,
in my world there is no finer bed, now I'm really tempted here to stay

> but nature of course reminded Him, of all He
> had still to do,
> like the wind, and rain, and that Adam thing,
> to mention just a few,

when God woke, after a well-earned rest, in His hand He took some
chalk,
and marked the spot that He had blessed and named it the city of
York,

> this tale I believe, you should take as
> read, that is, unless of course you know,
> where God did really rest His head,
> and then come to prove it so.

Jim Cuthbert

Heritage Of Richmond

Oh wondrous water dark and deep,
So perilous in your disguise,
Dark and foreboding, when seasons change,
Over boulders and reeds, where fish do leap,
If treated with contempt, then learn to despise,
Below its surface, hides, a terror that never wanes.

Upon its surface, twinkling, in sunbeams, and gurgles in sound,
Deep dark green banks reflected to shade its water life,
Early morning mists, chills in the air, the chatter of birds the silence
breaks,
You went your way, fast and slow, as each bend you flow around,
In the shadow of the castle, from times of drums and fife,
Peace and love, sport and leisure, to us you relate.

What secrets lie within your bed, arms and armour rusted and spent,
Building blocks, rubble and mortar from a distant life,
Bottles and jars from a misspent youth, dropped to float,
Hunters scour your bed to satisfy their bent,
Hints of medieval life, tantalise, and add spice,
If only you could relate, your hidden past, and quote.

Oh mighty river, symbol of the north, so proud and devious,
Of the victims you have claimed, due to their ignorance,
Did you weep and sympathise, for those you took their all,
The sound of thunder, in full flash flood, is disastrous,
Uprooted trees, debris and damage passes, as if in dance,
To stroll your banks, to stand and watch, to touch your water.

You the majesty of rivers, epitamy of the north,
Rugged, wild, deep and treacherous,
Calm, tranquil, warm, with petals and leaves on surface,
Sharp steps of rock, smooth rounded boulders on your course,
Shallow in places, over pebbles and weed you pass,
Oh wondrous Swale through Richmond, Yorks, you wend your way.

   T W Potter

SOUTH YORKSHIRE

The Visitor

If you're travelling into Doncaster
Approaching from the north
You'll see many, many changes
As you are going forth
They've built new roads and superstores
Where the green fields used to be
It seems so very different
For the likes of you and me
And when you reach the North Bridge
With its lights all shining bright
You'll enter into Frenchgate
Which is a lovely sight
They've put in seats and shrubs and trees
And altered all its style
But it's nice for tired shoppers
Just to rest awhile
Now as you enter the centre
With its many shops galore
It's nice to have a lovely day out
If you've never been there before
And if you are not very mobile
And your legs are not too sound
There are wheelchairs you can borrow
To help you to get around
It's a place to meet your old friends
To chat about the past
And for many, many pensioners
They've found friendship that will last
So if you're pleased with what you've seen
And you've really had a ball
There are all the shops you really need
So who needs *Meadow Hall?*

And if you're feeling tired
And you've seen all you want to see
Just stroll into a cafe
To have a lovely cup of tea
And now that your day is over
There's no one to complain
You'll look up at the Frenchgate Centre
Saying ~ I'd love to come here again

Vera Mosley

Memories of Greystones Cinema, Ecclesall Road, Sheffield

Probably the most memorable of all my childhood recollections is of the wonderful times spent at our local cinema which was called Greystones Picture Palace, situated in Ecclesall Road, Sheffield, a clean and well cared for cinema where I spent many happy hours with my parents. We would visit there once or twice a week according to the popularity of the films being shown at the time. I think, if I remember correctly, that it used to cost around 1/- (5p) for children and 1/9d (9½p) for adults, and that was for the best seats. Eventually the prices were increased to 1/3d (6½p) and 2/6d (12½p) respectively.

Greystones Cinema revolved around three people who virtually ran it, Vera, Bob and Raymond who made it a place of good family entertainment. We had known all of them for many years as my mother used to go to the cinema with her parents too, when she was a child. Raymond was the cinema projectionist and was always extremely smart, wearing rather elegant clothing with suede shoes, and was a confirmed bachelor who lived with his mother. Raymond was an awfully nice man, kind and polite, and often after the film had finished, he would invite us to go and have a friendly chat with him in the projection room which was hardly much bigger than the ladies loo. We were often late in arriving at the cinema, especially on cold winter evenings when we found great difficulty in drawing ourselves away from the blazing coal fire at home. Even if the box-office had closed however, we only had to go and knock on the door of the manageress's office to obtain our tickets, and then we would hurry upstairs to the balcony where the usherette would always manage to find us good seats, even though in those days the cinema was nearly always filled to capacity. During the film the 'ice-cream girl' would come round. That was Vera who was fifty if she was a day, about fifteen stones, with rouge-pink cheeks, and long blonde hair with a red rose planted firmly on top. Vera, who reminded one of a rather faded Mae West, could always be seen rushing up the road every evening, dressed in a long brown shabby raincoat and thick lyle stockings round equally thick legs, to start work at the cinema where, once inside, a complete transformation of her appearance took place, and she positively glowed as she came alive for a few hours like the rest of us, in another world far removed from reality. There again, like Raymond, Vera was an exceptionally kind soul who would do anything for anybody. The funniest of all was Bob, the odd-job man, commissionaire, and car-park attendant rolled into one. Bob was getting on in years, a small rotund little man about seventy, who looked just like one of the seven dwarfs. People rarely took much notice of Bob when he was directing the cars out of the parking area behind the cinema as he waved everybody on in spite of the fact that traffic would be coming both ways, and if one had taken notice of Bob's directions it could have proved quite disastrous. I remember with much amusement how between the houses (first and second showing of the film for those not familiar with cinema jargon) Bob would sit on the staircase leading up to the balcony, smoking a pipe. As mentioned previously, we were sometimes late and would be rushing up the stairs and were suddenly met with the drifting aroma of 'St Bruno' tobacco smoke and would frequently almost trip over him. He would merely look up nonchalantly and say, 'Hurry up now, King's nearly on,' joking in that dry humour peculiar to Northerners, and meaning that it was almost time to go home by the time we got there, as in those days they used to play the National Anthem at the end of the evening's film screening, and King George the VI was on the throne at the time. His facetious remarks caused much hilarity, and nothing can replace these special memories that dear old Greystones Cinema holds for me. The cinema was opened on July 27th 1914, but sadly due to the decline in audiences it finally closed its doors on August 17th 1968. Many years later in November 1982, after remaining empty and disused since it closed, the derelict building was ravaged by fire and was eventually demolished. The demise of the Greystones Cinema heralded the closure of the majority of cinemas across Sheffield and one felt that the curtain had finally been brought down on the glamorous era of the silver screen. It is a great shame that all the many wonderful original cinemas with their unique, ornate, and elegant interiors are now sadly no more and lost for all time due to demolition.

Susan Richardson

Remembering

I remember Bentley, the place where I was born,
The large and airy council house, with the big front lawn.
The playing field behind the house, where we had so much fun,
The local school not far away, to which we used to run.

The familiar sound of pit boots, of miners off to work,
To do their stint, in the bowels of the Earth.
Black faces returning, when the shift was o'er,
Sadly the mine is closed now, still and silent forever more.

Childhood memories often haunt me, remembering one sad day,
When a pit disaster shocked the village, and took my dad away.
Forty-five men and boys, lost their lives that fateful day.

The pleasant village of Arksey, about a mile away,
The fish pond where men can fish all day.
The level crossing where trains go by, to places far away.
The cemetery, where stands a memorial, to brave miners of yesterday.

Bentley Park where children play, the slides, swings, the fun.
Flower beds in summer, delight the eye with pride.
Bowling greens where men meet, to enjoy their game and sun.
The Pavilion stands so stately, is where we used to dance.

We left that village years ago, and went to Barnby Dun.
But still a part of me remains, in that place.
The terraced house in Cooke Street, where we started married life.
When I remember Bentley, thoughts light up my face.

Doris May Kitching

The Village Fair

Every year, wartime of course excepted, rain or shine, it came to most villages around (and suburbs of) Sheffield . . . the 'Feast'.

Eagerly anticipated by the children, 'Whoopee' for teenagers and tolerated by local residents. 'Feast' or 'Fair', the very word evokes wonderful memories of yesteryear fun ~ those 'hills' and 'valleys' of the Noah's Ark, negotiating the Cakewalk, regular pile-ups on the Dodgems.

Rides powered by electricity produced by the dynamo atop a mighty traction engine whose vibrations shook the earth upon which they stood. Clouds of black acrid smoke belching from chimneys. Fair organs playing tunes of the times. Lads 'eyeing' the Can-Can girls! Myriads of twinkling multicoloured light bulbs. Whizzing down the Helter Skelter and shrieks from the tilting 'Shamrock' boats.

Kiddies swings, penny-in-the-slot machines, rifle ranges, rolling coppers, darts, hoopla, immovable coconuts! 'Revelation's of the fortune tellers, 'Try your strength' machines, Romany Caravans ~ ponies grazing beside. Freak shows, the Bioscope, the man on stilts. Ice-cream, brandy snap, mushy peas, candy floss. Fairings for the girls ~ perhaps a kiss and a cuddle. And much, much more.

Happy days, perhaps brought to a successful conclusion with fish and chips for mum and the kids and a welcome pint for dad ~ now 'broke'! On the way home.

Joe Castle

Doncaster, Its Magic Seat

Waiting, it's a skill learned, as we grow older, waiting for demob, waiting to see a Doctor ~ Dentist, Birth, Death and, even a bus or holiday. Waiting for the wife, that's how I found the Magic Seat, I had to stand a while for someone else to move before claiming the seat.

'Sit there,' she said, 'I won't be long, keep hold of them there bags, you never know who's about.' She disappeared into the crowd, I breathed a sigh of relief! As I placed the shopping bags on the seat, they weighed heavy.

It wasn't long before it started to happen, not that I knew straight away. This large man took a seat next to me. 'How do?' he said, grinning quickly as his mouth turned into a sneer. 'Has thy ever had one of those days?' Pausing he stared into the crowd whilst giving a powerful belch, which polluted the area for a good ten yards around. I could not think of an answer to this, beside I was holding my breath against the beery smell. The smart looking woman at the other end of the seat disappeared. I was now feeling a bit itchy but my shopping bags formed a barrier between my new-found friend and I. Two police women, holding one elbow high, gripping some device at their waist belts, quite nice in their smart uniforms appeared in the distance, smiling and talking to each other, I turned to my companion, but marvellous! He also had disappeared.

Old Fred Smith raced by. Last time I met him he could not get about at all. He looked a bit dangerous weaving through the busy shoppers. This used to be his favourite seat ~ maybe this is where his miracle had happened. A nice old lady sat by my side. Smiling, she said, 'I'm waiting for our Hilda, she's down there.' She was looking along the street at some invisible person. Marvellous, I thought, it's the seat working again. She continued, 'I had to leave her when I saw him,' she said. 'He won't have owt to do with her if he sees me.' She struggled to her feet and walked away, soon to be lost in the crowd.

I had to move my shopping bags to make room for a youngish looking couple, probably in their sixties. 'I'm off t' toilet, I won't be long,' he said. The lady nodded, smiling at me, twisting her lips into a smart smirk, eyes opening a bit wider. 'I've only come to town today to get me 'air done. Cost me two pound fifty.' She turned her head, not wanting to be surprised by her man. 'I give lass two fifty for her sen.' She hesitates as if totalling it up. 'He has his done every eight weeks, but I manage to snip him, a bit round back in between, it saves a couple of pounds. I keep him happy though, when I come to town. I always go tuther end for his sweets, it's a long way,' she said, rubbing her thighs as she spoke. 'Keeps 'im happy, cheap shop that.' A strong perfume surrounded us, it's the seat again I thought, only to be corrected by the lady speaking to her returning man. 'Tha's been round them scent counters agen,' looking towards me, shaking her head. 'Let's be off, see thee later, bye!' she said. They too disappeared into the crowd, leaving me wondering whether I needed a haircut.

The sunlight felt warm, I closed my eyes and relaxed. A bus passed by, its large wheels swishing. Opening my eyes into the dream I saw the large double decker maroon bus, the conductor leaning out of the door, guiding people, shouting, 'Move along, please, plenty of room on top.' With a loud ding-ding it moved off, with sparking wires above, passing shoppers, drably dressed in dark clothing. A hunger-creating smell drifted into the street from the sausage shop. My dried mouth dropped open. 'Wake up, thee daft bat, where's bags?' Shaken out of the magic, I reached behind the seat and stumbled into a brighter light of colourfully dressed people. Joining them we disappeared.

If you find the seat, be careful! You never know who's about!

Roy Barker

Doncaster, Circa 2000

My town has changed so very much,
Since my long lost days of youth,
For the better? You may ask,
But I don't think so, that's the truth.

A community, once proud,
Torn asunder by recession,
Redundancies and closures,
Leading workers to depression.

Where coal was king, now nothing,
The pitheads stand forlorn,
No longer will those proud men
Work the seams to earn their corn.

The factories are all but gone,
And in their place today,
What do we have to offer?
Not a lot, my friends, I'd say!

A soulless town, not what it was,
Even the shops have changed.
The special, little shops have left,
The whole town centre rearranged.

We can't drive down the High Street,
Cars aren't wanted in the town.
The buses aren't too cheap,
They really know how to bring us down!

Our parks, once green and vibrant,
Now appear in some decay.
Facilities for leisure
Cost too much for most to pay.

Is this really progress?
Just what will the future hold?
More 'improvement', more 'development'?
My friends, it leaves me cold!

Brian L Porter

South Yorkshire Sorties

For a view of South Yorkshire for one and all
try walking from Blackburn to Meadowhall.
Here the modern with the older age mix
you see it all in a huge 'pick and mix'!

If it's snowdrops you would rather see
then Roche Abbey is the place for me.
Standing, trembling, pale and green ~
a lovelier sight you've never seen!

What about Hoober covered in grime!
The Follies have stood for a very long time.
Years of coal dust have taken their toll,
but interesting too, if you want a stroll.

Have you been to Turner Wood?
Along the paths where horses trod.
Quiet and rural, tranquil and green,
with ducks and boats ~ a pastoral scene.

Bustling markets and folk that are *real*
exist where used to be iron and steel.
Beside the motorway, culture and leisure,
look right, look left, hours of pleasure.

Hilary M Rose

In The Rotherham Town

I walked down to the Rotherham town,
Even though I should have took the Mainline bus.

Superdrug, Woolworths, and Body Care,
Sell beauty products, this and that for hair.
Primark, New Look, Top Shop, The Bay,
Buy your clothes from here today.
Going Places, Thomas Cook, Lunn Poly too.
They'll make your holiday dreams come true.
Yorkshire Bank, Lloyds Bank, Abbey National for you,
Get a loan, cash a cheque, put money in them too.
Heart Foundation, Cancer Research, Oxfam, PDSA,
Charities full of second-hand goods to blow the mind away.
Dragon Pearl, Mail Coach Inn, Dunkby's, Tutem Shive,
Pop in for a beer or two, or coffee in the café.

I walked out of the Rotherham town,
Even though I should have took the Mainline bus.

Michelle Taylor

Sheffield

I tell a tale of Sheffield
its history and its past
its world-wide fame for making steel
which up to now does last

Mary, Queen of Scots, came here
at Manor Castle stayed
some fourteen years imprisoned
later with her life paid

Who can forget ow'd Charlie Peace
a murderer for sure
but yet the story of him
has passed into folklore

Queen Victoria came here
o'er hundred years ago
her presence here in Sheffield
caused patriotic glow

Then in nineteen thirty-five
Wednesday won the cup
Ronnie Starling shoulder high
did proudly lift it up!

Then came t' Blitz and wartime
this city played its part
Churchill praised the loyal hearts
that stood firm and stalwart

So much more could be said
of those who lived and died
the famous and the unsung
in t' city of civic pride!

Kenny Raymond

House Renovations At Tinsley, Sheffield

The fifties were flushed out of you
not slowly in response to
market forces but in one mass exorcism.

A plague of youths, hobnailed and fag
dangling descended on you
like locusts or some species of burrowing

beetle intent on a breakfast
of dry rot and damp wallpaper.

And before you were able to catch that breath
that exhilaration born of unburdening
a new age was cemented into windowspaces

and new roofs contained the civic
aspirations of tomorrow's world.

Now you are old without history;
smart without learning;
lively without living
and fit to play egg to dead chickens
awaiting revival in scarred
and empty acres across the way.

Tony Noon

Back Then

I wur nowt but a lad when I went darn pit
And I can tell thee I wur really scared
'Nar dunt thee go cryin' when wi get t' pit'
Mi dad said. As if I would've dared

When I got t' pit bottom I were shakin'
And deputy said, 'Dunt thee worry, young lad
Thar in a good team t' start wi.'
Turns art the best mates that I had

I 'eard language I thought nivver existed
Which couldn't be repeated above ground
Mi fingers wur bleedin', mi back hurt like hell
All that for less than a pound

On afternoons when sun wur shinin'
It broke me 'eart t' get int cage
I can't miss a shift or mi mates would go mad
And week after I'd be short in mi wage

I nivver got used t' goin' darn that black 'ole
Even after thirty-nine years
Sum days were filled wi laughter
And others ended in tears

Back then wi were a proper community
Just goin' abart ar daily task
And if ever tha wanted a favour
All tha'd t' do wur just ask

But nardays it's all a different
And things 'ave changed quite a lot
They all want t' be better than each other
Instead of bein' happy wi what they've got

It's young uns that I feel sorry for
There's no work abart for them t' do
They'll 'ave no werkmates t' call on
Only them they stand wi in dole queue

I wouldn't like t' bring back them owd days
But there's summat missin' today
Nobody's got time for each other
They all just go their own way

Today there's no sense of commitment
Not even t' them tha calls friend
No takin' pride int community
Seems all that's come to an end

Workin' darn pit it was murder
But camaraderie wur second t' none
Now that coal industry's no longer
I'm afraid that friendship's long gone

Peter Wilson

The Vigil Of St Mark's
(St Mark's Eve 24th April. Wath Parish Churchyard)

If you stand alone when the moon is pale
at the midnight hour, by the churchyard rail.
Out of sight in some corner dark,
on that mystic night ~ the eve of Saint Mark,
When the year is right; which is one in three
a terrible sight you are like to see.

For down the path from the churchyard gate
may well be seen by those who dare to wait,
A grim procession from the street
each one clothed in a winding sheet;
One by one at a solemn pace
each with a candle to light its face.

Here be the great and here the small
soon to lie 'neath a funeral pall,
For everyone processing here
is due to die in the coming year.
On they go to the open the door,
And thence inside, to be seen no more.

So beware observer lest you spy
your own dark spirit passing by.

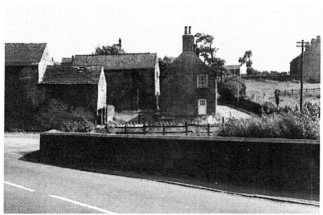

Janet Cavill

159

Steel

My husband's in the steelworks, he drives a crane all day
he tells me he works very hard, to earn his meagre pay.

He sits and pushes levers, he had to do it right,
'cos when he's got the ladle on, the steel is boiling white.

He has to drop the moulds in, whatever they may be,
and swinging chains with dogs on, is a sight I'd like to see.

He has to stack the ingots, they're for the Mill next door,
and when that lot is on its way, he has to stack some more.

He has to do a Rack out, and I think he swings a hook,
and I know they clean the pans out, but I'm not sure what they cook.

They have to put a stopper in, and it has to fit,
or else they get a runner, and the steel goes down the pit.

I tell him these expressions, don't sound as though they're real,
but he tells me I'll get used to it. I'm married into *steel.*

Aline Westwood